Also by Susie Bright

Coauthor with Jill Posener, *Nothing But the Girl: The Blatant Lesbian Image*

Sexwise

Susie Bright's Sexual Reality: A Virtual Sex World Reader

Susie Sexpert's Lesbian Sex World

Editor, *Herotica, Herotica 2, Herotica 3*

Editor, *The Best American Erotica, 1993–1997*

Susie Bright's Sexual State of the Union

♀ ♂ ♀ ♂ ♀ ♂ ♀ ♂

Susie Bright

SIMON & SCHUSTER

SIMON & SCHUSTER
Rockefeller Center
1230 Avenue of the Americas
New York, NY 10020

SIMON & SCHUSTER and colophon are registered trademarks of
Simon & Schuster Inc.

Designed by Irving Perkins Associates

Manufactured in the United States of America

10   9   8   7   6   5   4   3   2   1

Library of Congress Cataloging-in-Publication Data

Bright, Susie, date.
    [Sexual state of the union]
    Susie Bright's sexual state of the union / Susie Bright.
      p.   cm.
    Includes bibliographical references and index.
    1. Sex customs—United States.   2. Sex (Psychology).   I. Title.
HQ18.U5B754   1997
306.7—dc21   96-44603
                                         CIP

ISBN 0-684-80023-3

Acknowledgments

My deepest gratitude to:

The Nitty-Gritty Elephant Team: my heroic agents and managers Jo-Lynne Worley and Joanie Shoemaker; my partner and One-Man Tactical Squad, Jon Bailiff; my breaking-all-previous-records editor, the breathtaking and illuminating Bethany Clement; the miracle known as Ari Levenfeld, my editorial and production assistant; my friend and comrade in book-writing hell, Lisa Palac; my father and best editor, Bill Bright; Honey Lee Cottrell, for her ever-present support and knowledge; and my tireless editor at Simon & Schuster, Cynthia Gitter.

Invaluable Counsel: Mike Godwin, Brock Meeks, Sandy Berman, Mark Chimsky, Andrew Rice, Shar Rednour, Chris Mann, Jeff Armstrong, Tony Lovett, Jared Rutter, Doug Oliver, Jill Posener, Jack Morin, Nancy Stoller, Carter Wilson, The Well, Constance Penley, Linda Williams, Michael Letwin, my UCSC students, Gayle Rubin, Sally Binford, Laura Miller, Aretha Bright, and Rebecca Hall.

Last, But Hardly Least: Spain Rodriguez, Susan Stern, Betty Dodson, Max Valerio, Evelyn McDonnell, Adrienne Landry, Willy Grover, Ann Powers, Alex & Elsa MacAdams, Victor Castro, and the alumni of *On Our Backs,* Good Vibrations, Caught Looking, and Mainstream Exiles.

To my Aunt Molly

Contents

Contents

Sex Toys

On the Road

Totally Offensive

Introduction

The Wrong Question

Lust brings out the liar in everyone. Every erection has Pinocchio written up and down its length—yes, everybody wants to be REAL, a real boy, an honest woman, unafraid and upright—but then desire, the ultimate honesty, does us in. Desire doesn't give a whit about shame. Our secrets, our exaggerations and distractions, it's all just a lot of twisting in the wind as far as sex is concerned—what we want WILL come out.

When we talk about sex to each other, one-on-one, we open a well-worn box of lovers' lies: fake orgasms, promises of fidelity, boastful exploits. But on a social stage, lying about sex grows to such a grandiose level that instead of just answering with fibs and false-hoods, our collective breath doesn't even pose an honest question. The very premises of our education, our media, our aesthetics, as-sume tremendous beliefs about sexuality that aren't any more real than a flat earth. Instead, double standards and things that go bump in the night are the order of the day, the order of our childhoods, our daily bread.

My childhood was filled with pious and common messages about sin, femininity, romance, and virginity. I'm glad the nuns in my parochial school took off their habits; that was "the beginning of the end," just like the pope predicted. It was the sixties, we let our hair

11

down, and the lies about good girls and bad girls fell from our heads like useless hairpins. I learned what the word "hypocrisy" meant in those years, what a social lie can do to a person. It made a tremendous impression on me, especially when I'm confronted with some of the whoppers that are served up today.

Today, I see a magazine headline that impeaches pregnant teenagers for their promiscuity and irresponsible decision making—what a tough little accusation that is. Everyone who actually works with pregnant teenagers or is related to a pregnant teenager—not to mention a pregnant teenager herself—knows that the girl-teen was probably knocked up by a full-grown man who is way past his adolescent angst. These men, these fathers, are like ghosts, who go unmentioned by the politician or the talk show host.

It would be interesting, of course, to find out how many of our social critics and leaders have had sex with teenagers themselves—or had sex when they WERE teenagers. But that's not the question being asked. We don't ask political pundits about their sex lives: we listen to them question ours. The result? Something as idiotic as the Bad Teen Question hangs around like a foul smell, a blame game with a voiceless target.

Blame 'n' Shame is the spinning bottle of sexual politics. It's such a winner because it covers all the essentials with a mountain of blankets, each embroidered with somebody else's sins. The naked truth, when it drags up questions that are not doused with shame and blame, is usually not as attractive to the public appetite—it doesn't fit the *"How could you?!"* agenda.

"I could, and I did, and you would too, if you had half a chance" is the answer that bears repeating, but it takes a lot of guts to say it out loud. The class yell of the sexually repressed society—"Tha---at's sick!"—is an appropriate insult from those who put sex and pathology in the same bed. We know how to say no to sex in fifty different languages, in every mood, place, and time, but it's clear why it rings so hollow and aching sometimes—we never learned to say yes to sex, without duress, without a fall from grace.

Disease, in particular the specter of AIDS in our current consciousness, is a virtual geyser of opportunities for people to make moral conclusions out of ignorance. The fear-mongers' sense of righteousness and revenge is so cruel and omnipresent that even those who do become sick and helpless may turn on themselves and say, "What have I done to deserve this?"

Nothing, nothing at all.

"What have I done?" is not the real question. What has stopped us from discovering the origins of HIV—a far better and more difficult question—is not lack of money but lack of consciousness. We've been so busy praying for special favors and redemption, feeling unique, posting the blame, that the truth and the mysteries of our bodies become ever more elusive. Someday there's likely to be a scientific explanation for AIDS, and as with every great epidemic, people will look at the past and sigh, "If only it hadn't been for the politics—it was right under our noses." The "fag disease" has nothing to do with men desiring other men. In both plagues, transmission and proximity—your zip code—have had nothing to do with grace.

Sex is such an urgent message from our body that sometimes we call it our soul. Lust carries risks, sexual intimacy has consequences; it IS nature, not a gadget with a warranty. Nobody would go through it if the rewards were not so magnificent: the knowledge of one's body, the basic connection with another person. Without eroticism there is no love: even love between parent and child begins with such bliss, the end of the spectrum that begins at nurture and need. The most outstanding result of lust is new life, both in real births and in the birth of our creativity, and such events are nothing short of a sensation. Of course it's worth it, and what's more, what the puritans and their gong shows don't seem to realize is that it's inevitable. Their prudery is killing people, both metaphorically and literally, but they cannot mandate their vision of purity because it is, at its very core, an affront to our survival.

The ills and superstitions of our erotic poverty have been an enormous burden to bear. Double-talk and the bogeyman are the staples of public sexual debate. Someone is always trying to shut someone else up when it comes to sex, trying to keep it "out of the home," when it should be perfectly obvious that sex is home, *chez nous*—we don't need an outside line.

Now that technology spawns new litters of communication devices like rabbits, there are plenty of jobs and speaking opportunities for the censorship-minded. The latest burn-and-ban crusade takes place on the Internet, the marvel of millions of people gathered together on the same party line. What an opportunity to connect with a perfect stranger, to talk about perfect sex, to even have virtual sex on line! Yet if the censors have their way—our elected leaders, our school boards and administrators, our captains of media and entertainment—only THEY will get to stay on the line, while everyone else is going to have their toe tagged if they get caught thinking and talking about something that somebody else doesn't like.

The critical issue here isn't SEX, the issue is ELITISM. Some people think they are morally and intellectually qualified to view everything and then decide what's appropriate for the peasants. They talk about protecting children, with "children" as a code word for anyone they consider their inferior.

Last year I read an article by Marcelle Lean, a woman who sat for six years on the Ontario Film Board, a privileged group of prominent citizens who check out every new film entering the province. After viewing each movie, this group has a discussion about the film's merits, whether it should be seen by other Canadians, and whether any warnings should be carried along with its release. Her story revealed that she is part of the most fascinating weekly movie discussion group in the country. She adores movies and she loves to discuss them with a similarly motivated group. Her board has intense debates about sex, violence, role models, and politics—and she considers herself a more enriched person because of it, even when her opinion doesn't carry the majority.

At some point, Lean had to wonder aloud what it would be like if everyone in Ontario were allowed to have the same freedom of discussion that she enjoys! But this was a moot point; the people of Ontario were being treated like children who cannot be allowed to make a meal for themselves because they'll surely burn down the house.

The same situation exists in the United States, although the chain of bureaucracy is different. We have the Motion Pictures Rating Board, which reigns like an imperial wizard over the fortunes of any film's potential distribution. The fear of what the MPRB will censor and consequently suppress is so omnipresent that moviemakers take it upon themselves to precensor their content, and actors take it upon themselves to precensor what roles they will play, and so on down the line, until all we are left with is the pabulum and toothless clichés that pass for entertainment.

Now ratings are coming to television, and we are to receive a little content-buster called a V-chip that has the capability to scan and filter out things as banal as whether an actress takes off her top. After all, we know what the sight of nipples can do to a civilized society! Such discriminations are exasperating. If I serve someone a remarkable meal, would it be appropriate for them to inquire whether I was wearing my underwear or not? My own daughter asks that question at mealtime occasionally, but she's only six, so it's good for a laugh; we forgive her for being preoccupied with what she thinks of as daring sexual knowledge. Little does she know that her perceptions would qualify her as a new ratings commissar.

Some false premises about sexuality have had such a devastating

15

effect that discussions and philosophies that were once meaningful have been turned into laughingstocks. Feminism as an intellectual movement has been largely torpedoed by stupid sex questions. The last time I was at a feminist symposium, surrounded by magnificent female minds, our host opened up the discussion by asking, "Can a feminist wear lipstick?" She almost lost the whole group of us right there and then. Feminism is not about whether you're going to be cute or doggy, fucked or unfucked, nice or mean to the other girls. Feminists have gouged each other on such questions because they've been in a closet as big and crowded as all of Macy's basement. But until every last woman comes out about her sexual desire, it's going to be a bloody mess.

Why are some women trying to slap chastity belts on their sisters? Is this a movement of reform, or a B-movie reform school? Nothing reminds a woman more of her second-class status than having her daddy AND her big sisters tell her what to do.

Politics today is nothing so much as the politics of infantilism—and they're by far the meanest, nastiest group of babies we've seen in a long time. Not only is everyone accusing everyone else of being a big baby ("You whiner! You victim!"), but finger-pointing aside, there is also a driving need for a true collective BABY—an infant to protect, a child to scold, an innocent to titillate the adult public's worst fears. When grown-ups get scared about sex, they say, "What about the children?" instead of the more truthful "What about me?" Those who aren't holding the reins are treated like they belong in a precocious romper room, where they can be saved, preached to, punished, or made exceptions of. This is America's playpen.

Sure, there's an appeal to naming political dynamics the way one does family members, but here's the thing: there are flesh-and-blood children who need food, comfort—and power. The politics of infantilism doesn't speak to them at all. Their presence is barely acknowledged, their names are spoken only in rhetoric. We have fetishized childhood and all its sentiments on our sacrificial altars, folded them in to our titillating little taboos—but this has nothing to do with taking care of our own.

After I gave birth to my daughter, I was flush with nest-making and Mommy-ness, but I also found myself withdrawing a bit from other friends' problems and concerns. I had been so involved with trying to help So-and-So make the right decision that my change of direction hit me hard. Here I had a real baby who truly did need me to protect and guide her in the most elemental way, while my grown-up friends are, in the end, going to do what they damn well please. If I raise my daughter well, she will grow up to be just as independent as my peers. She lies in my arms for such a short amount of time. I have to be humble about this.

Reality does temper all our sexual perceptions, and when I rant about just how WRONG the world can be about sex, it's more than a little presumptuous to imagine that my small band of bohemians and I were handed the one true word. It's not like that.

Sexual perceptions, those false premises, are formed by ignorance, pure and desperate. It's not only the troubling things we don't understand today, but also the superstitions of years past that cling to all the dark places where people don't get information, don't get examples, don't get an opportunity to try out anything different. I'm not talking about a cave, I'm talking about everything and everyone—from entire states in this country where you can't get simple information about sexuality, to a Los Angeles radio station manager who handed me a piece of paper that said, "Please do not use the word *clitoris*." That's the legacy of censorship and elitism: we are erased below the waist, in the interest of the so-called public welfare—an interest so narrowly defined that it rules out just about everyone who doesn't own their own cable company or have a chair on the FCC.

Is our sexuality a basic, good, and precious thing that somehow became terribly misunderstood? Or is there something really evil out there in Sex Land that attaches itself to our libidos, and is only held back by vigilance and caution?

We are closest to a pessimistic answer when we are touched by the news of a sexual criminal, a nut job, the person whose sadism and lack of compassion not only leads him to rape and murder but seemingly out of the human realm. We call such people monsters, and what does that say about us?

> *No beast so fierce but knows some touch of pity.*
> *But I know none, and therefore am no beast.*
>
> —SHAKESPEARE, *RICHARD III*

Our fears of the monsters, the incomprehensible beasts, are so alienated and unexamined from our own life experiences that it leads me to believe that, at heart, the monsters are our own making. We know these aberrations were once in diapers sucking their thumbs; so what happened? We beg for God to answer this question. Our leaders and experts get out bibles and manuals and statistics, but instead of getting answers, we just get static—"Pornography and the devil made me do it." Our monsters, and our own monstrous feelings, have not been touched one iota by this kind of rationalization. We don't understand sexual power at all.

I'm thought of as a person who is optimistic about sex, someone who thinks of sexual knowledge as salvation and inspiration, not a one-way ticket to Babylon. Ignorance is blissful—I know that—and it is harder to KNOW that you don't understand, that nobody knows the answers, and still to be optimistic about the sexual state of the union. That's why there aren't any joyful existentialists.

There are only the soul artists, the hedonists, the flower people of our age, kissing the ground and loving every minute of it. The ground could open up and swallow us, it could freeze our asses off, you could be struck by lightning just as the blossom touches your lips. Sex is weather, sex is mother nature; I don't have to call myself an optimist to love her—I guess I could just say I keep my eyes and my liar's mouth open in awe.

Good Breeding

My First Dirty Picture

CARTOONIST ROBERT CRUMB TOLD me that the first dirty picture he ever saw was a ten-second glimpse of something his older brother was circulating on the playground. Big brother was subsequently caught pink-handed and suspended. "It was a naked lady," Robert recalls, "with great big tits."

Female masturbation guru Betty Dodson, who's older than Robert but of the same generation, told me she drew her own first dirty picture. Furthermore, she got away with it. Betty remembers that her girlfriends dared her. They said she didn't know how a man and woman did it. She said, "Do so!" and dashed off a man with an enormous dick entering a woman with an equally huge vagina. She surprised herself.

I grew up in the sixties, and my first dirty picture was a photograph. I discovered it when I was in fifth grade, playing around after school off Baldwin Avenue, a suburban main drag in the San Gabriel Valley. I was scoping out one of several undeveloped lots. People dumped stuff there; I found all kinds of garbage treasures they'd discarded, and I also used it as a site to hide my best clothes. I left early for school every morning to make a quick change on the road after my mother had approved my attire. This was 1968, and I had two se-

cret skirts that my mother had thrown away but I had rescued because they were finally short enough. She wanted my skirts down to
my knees. She wanted me to wear saddle shoes, too. But I had a pair
of Adidas stashed in one particular tree. I liked to find new places for
future stashes.

Those Adidas represented wishful thinking: not only did I have
secret clothes, I also had secret friends, girls who would no more
want to be seen with me, an unpopular brain, on campus, than I
would want to be seen in Oxfords.

Jessie Nelder was a friend like that. She was cool; she had long
blond ironed hair and paisley mini-dresses. Her parents were hippies
who put marijuana in their spaghetti sauce, and she really liked to
hang out with me—AFTER school hours. We were both aficionados
of *Harriet the Spy*, scavengers of vacant lots and garbage dumps.

There was one thicket of bushes on this particular vacant lot
that was perfect for hiding, ideal for spying. It was a fort of thick
prickles with an empty space inside, a dusty nest. We found it on a
spring afternoon, just before the early smog alert days. We loved it.
Jessie and I picked through it expertly, and I said, "I feel like I'm in a
mouse cage, this place is filled with shredded Kleenex."

I kicked away at the muddy tissues, and then I found the prize.
It was a shoebox-size black patent leather purse. It was shiny and
perfect for dress-up, and when I unsnapped the gold buckle, I exposed a soft peach satin lining. Jessie grabbed it from me, and a
handful of Polaroids fell out.

"Shit," she said. I didn't say anything. The first photo I looked
at was a man's body, overexposed and yellow, wearing a bra, holding
his penis. The white straps crossing his jaundice-colored chest disturbed me right off the bat, and I could only look at his dick out of
the corner of my eyes. In contrast to his shiny limbs, it looked like a
big red hot dog. I wouldn't eat hot dogs for quite a while after that.

All the pictures had the same man in women's underwear, and
some of them had a woman taking his penis in her mouth. I can't be

certain what the woman was doing in the photographs because I couldn't hold still to give them a second look. One glimpse at that skinny man in a brassiere and I was trembling. I was sure he was coming back, he was coming back any minute, he was crazy, he would kill us.

Jessie was absolutely unconcerned about what he was going to do to us, and totally exhilarated about what we were going to do to HIM. She was the one who claimed the woman was "performing fellatio." I'd never heard that word before, and when she said it, it appeared as a bubble in my head: "filet-show"—some sort of horrible show.

There was also a tube of red lipstick in the purse. I remember that shade of lipstick more than anything else; it was flaming. Jessie, the eagle eye, noticed that it was the same color that the man was wearing on his lips in the picture. "We'll show him!" she said, and started to squish the soft red wax into the ground.

"No, no!" I begged her, "What are you doing?" I wanted to leave everything as we had found it, without a trace of our presence.

"What am I doing?" Jessie said, excited even more by my desperation. "What is HE doing? HE's sick," she said, and with that inspiration she took what was left of the lipstick and scrawled "You're Sick" on the side of the patent leather purse.

"We'll never be able to come back here again," I said. If Jessie had read *Harriet the Spy* more carefully, she would have known that the whole point is to leave everything as it was, so you can come peek at it over and over again.

I went back to those bushes alone the next day. I was nervous, but I had to see if he had returned. The thicket had been cleared out. I was so angry at Jessie for scaring him away. I wanted to look at the pictures again; I'd somehow crossed from terrified sissy to persistent voyeur overnight. But there were only a few torn-up pieces of Kleenex left behind.

I had, on Baldwin Avenue, all the elements of a pornographic experience. I felt the secrecy, the excess, the fear of violent reactions, the quease of perversion.

"You're sick, I'm scared, he's going to pay, and the show is over before you know it." I think that's a pretty typical feminine experience of porn. I didn't look at another dirty picture until I was nineteen years old.

Little Faith

I WAS RAISED ROMAN Catholic, but the first church group that truly bowled me over was the Latter Day Saints. I was recruited on the playground by a little girl my own age, who boasted of her large family (very impressive to me, an only child) and the church extravaganzas, in which every member participated either on or off stage. Make no mistake about the singing Osmond family—they are the product of Mormon theatrical training. I loved to dance and sing and play-act, so I was delighted to accept her invitations to nightly rehearsals and trainings.

Education for youngsters in the church was action-packed. We sang our hearts out one night, and afterward, one of the adult leaders, an off-duty policeman, came in and showed us his sample drug collection. My first look at marijuana was a sprig of the plant in a little glass tube, which the officer encouraged us to open up and sniff. "Peeuuuw!" we all screamed. I was fascinated to learn about these dangerous drugs, so illegal and exotic. I asked the teacher what being high was like, and he compared it to spinning around in a circle until you lost your balance. The roomful of kids sprang to the auditorium floor for a simulated "getting high" exercise, all of us spinning, whirling dervishes in sneakers, screaming and laughing "I'm SO DIZZY" until the floor was littered with child-size dogpiles.

My Catholic catechism had been nothing this forward, this explicit. The raciest discussion I'd ever heard under the nuns' tutelage had been a rather stern but unbreathless description of the relationship between serial murderer Charles Manson and the use of an at-home Ouija board. The Mormons WERE breathless; they yelled at sins, they didn't whisper about them. It was the closest I've ever come to being on a professional sports team.

One day at the LDS church, the grown-ups separated the kids by gender and took a small group of girls into a little room. The volume level went way down, and it was clear that our petite teacher was going to speak to us more discreetly. She had a little chalkboard and marker to draw with, which she used to outline the figure of an arm—an underarm to be exact. "As you grow older, and become a woman, you are going to grow hair"—she paused—"under your arms, and also in other places. Hair under the arms is a sign of woman's original sin, and we do not let this shame be seen." She proceeded to talk about the danger of sleeveless blouses.

Some quick-thinking little protofeminist in our group asked the teacher why it was okay for the boys to show the hair under their arms, and this prompted an even more tangled lecture on what that little slut Eve had wrought upon mankind. I'd give anything to be able to quote that speech as easily as I remember her words about the unspeakable hair growth—but my attention had been snared by this introduction, and I couldn't concentrate further.

I knew, I knew for certain, that she was wrong about women's body hair. I knew there were millions of women around the world who had underarm hair who were living without sin or shame—flourishing even. I recognized her comments as being from someone who had never been let out of the house—the house being this particular church in Pasadena, California.

The whole Mormon philosophy started to unravel for me after that. I was pretty new to this feeling of superiority over an adult: I didn't have the nerve to say, "I may only be eight, but you are totally silly and misinformed." But the idea that she could be so superstitious, so wrong, and yet hold our group captive to her ignorance and prejudices—it made me sick to my stomach.

It still makes me sick to my stomach: America's tradition of religious intolerance, of scaring children, threatening women, and provoking men with its little poison-tipped arrows of bigotry and damnation. Sure I learned the golden rule, too, and the kindness of Jesus, and I sang "They Will Know We Are Christians by Our Love, by Our Love"—but who the hell recognizes Christians by their love anymore, if they ever did? Christians are meanies, like the other big religions of the world. They carry a big stick and a big book, and they make anyone who doesn't agree with them feel very, very small—ripe for colonization. Christianity is elitist, it's not democratic. It's about Our Father and everybody underneath him. I'll never get used to cute progressives referring to God as "she" or "it," because I know from every aspect of Catholic training I received that God is an angry, vengeful M-A-N.

Christianity is an ancient form of sex education, and, let's face it, its prophets got just about everything wrong. God is Butterfly Mc-Queen, running down the street screaming, "I don't know nothing 'bout birthing no babies!" Early Christians didn't understand the whys and wherefores of pregnancy, menstruation, birth, menopause, sexual fantasies, or desire; so instead we receive the myths, the admonitions about pubic hair. The church is notorious for condemning women as lesser creatures, as sewers—"saccus stercoris," a sack of shit, according to one early church father—and armpit hair is just one small manifestation of this attitude.

I don't usually speak this frankly of my revulsion with religion to my churchgoing friends. I'm acquainted with many folks who do believe in God—"some of my best friends." They find that their belief and their church community embraces tolerance and serenity and compassion. Some of my church-attending friends are the kind of people who'd invite me to their congregation to speak, who welcome female and gay clergy members, who feel that their role is to speak out and agitate for the most unfortunate and alienated members of society. I've visited convents that were more like guerrilla headquarters, gathering places for the bravest and most selfless women I've ever met. One friend of mine is the grandson of the man who invented "Dial A Prayer," and far from the kitschy connotations that such a project calls up, his family is a dedicated line of Presbyterians who feel it is their moral duty to offer comfort, empowerment, and spiritual aid to the communities where they live. No wonder church groups are just about the only place where grassroots organization of voters happens anymore—church is the last place that people gather to share their hopes and dreams as a community.

Yet as sympathetic as I feel to friends and family who find a progressive and nourishing space in their church, I know their place of worship will never play a part in the leadership of social change—at best, they will only reflect those changes. My own experience in the Catholic church included its painful response to the antiwar movement, its reaction to feminism, its informal recognition of gay clergy— but I could hardly hold the priests responsible. You cannot look at the history of the Catholic church and become idealistic about the place of women, authority, or peaceful coexistence. Churches that have survived the centuries have done so because of a very heavy thumb, and now that some of their members want to pick and choose what's appealing from a spiritual menu, their foundations are simultaneously ridiculed, obscured, and revered. How else can one explain the pope? In a sense, I sympathize with the fundamentalists, who look at the modern Protestant denominations—not to mention liberal Catholics and Jews—and write them off as irresponsible flakes. The liberal churches ARE guilty of revisionism, as realistic and progressive as their revisions are. It takes a real Noah's Ark mentality to stick to the old guns, because today the world is flooded with democratic and creative aspirations, frightening and provoking the patriarchs. For the God squad, you're either under siege or you're doing a rewrite.

How many times have I been invited to a friend's church or religious study group, with the irresistible line: "You don't even have to believe in God to join!" No, you DON'T have to believe in a God in heaven to have a meaningful spiritual community, and no one could seduce an intellectual with any different positions. But how many churches are willing to fearlessly repudiate their past, to pull up the floorboards? I'm sure it seems futile to them, an indulgent exercise in self-criticism when their ministry is pressed to attend to the community-building tasks and suffering at hand.

I'm just not sure they can have it both ways and see a revival. The notion that church members don't have to swallow the whole scripture and legacy of oppression only encourages members to keep questioning. If their leaders teach with utmost integrity, they will essentially lead their most search-oriented members right out of the church altogether. Good for them—but that's a tough thing to advertise. The Ministry of Truth that longs to set its members free!

For me, it's difficult to believe in God, but it comes naturally to believe in civilization, in common consciousness, in the future of humanity. I have my mysticism too, which cannot be entirely credited to science; in fact, I look at scientists as some of the most mystery-besotted citizens of all. It takes a lot to believe in things we can't see, and our self-interest can lead us to rationalize and defend the most outrageous claims.

Sex has been one of my litmus tests for faith. I can't go for religious gatherings that want to punish the sexual, despise it, claim that it's not human or worthy. Even the most liberal churches have been afraid of sexuality, mired in guilt, superstition, and the demands of churchgoing gender roles. Sexual creativity as a spiritual path, or a liberation of enlightenment, has singularly been reserved for pagans, the Bacchanalians—and you won't find them leading any interdenomination parade.

My religion-respecting comrades warn me that there's no strategic point in feeling superior to the conventionally faithful. They treat me like some diehard vegan who won't give the meat-eaters one teensy little break.

All right, as political strategy or just out of common courtesy, I agree with them. Acting like a snotty communist doesn't endear me to the spiritually sincere. My alienation provides tremendous distance and doubt. But here's the sticky part: I DO feel superior to deeply religious people, because I'm one of those who thinks they're smoking opium! I don't believe in their God or their Satan, and that kind of faith genuinely seems backward to me, a sign of ignorance and fear. I see their dedication and power, but the true believers might as well be worshipping a cheeseball as far as I'm concerned.

The loving, generous, and truth-demanding principles of Christianity and many other world religions are always deep-sixed for me because of their stipulated intolerance. Whether they want to save me because of compassion, or slay me for being an infidel, the policy of live and let live is ultimately not in the Holy Book vocabulary.

I resent having to button my lip about being a nonbeliever or a queer or a woman who's had abortions, or WHATEVER, just so they can see that we have other things in common. Why isn't it their responsibility to accommodate? Instead, reaction is their only response. My inclination has always been to free the fearful faithful from their isolation—maintained by geography and censorship—and let them experience all the millions of people in the world who don't believe the same way they do. Into the river, everyone! Isn't that why people like me left the church to begin with? I just needed someone to show me the exit sign out of the pews.

Good Breeding

THE DAY I BEGAN to menstruate was a terrible, horrible, no-good, very bad day. I knew what my period was; I didn't think I was dying, I didn't search for rags. I just got the tampon box out of my mother's cupboard and read the directions several times. They were good directions; I will always thank the writers at Tampax for making it perfectly clear how to stick one of these things in. I had heard that virgins were not supposed to use tampons, that you might hurt yourself and cause damage. But then I thought wearing one of those pads that was as big as my head might cause terrible damage too. The tampon slid inside my vagina without any pain, and all that was left to do was clean up all the blood on my clothes and the floor and the toilet.

I remember thinking how weird it was that girls did this every month, cleaning up blood. Since boys didn't do anything like it on a regular basis, it had to make for real loss of mutual understanding. But I didn't think about that for long. I was late for school, and the first person I told about my period wasn't my mother or a girlfriend but Mr. Shalka, the junior high principal. I marched into his office after the bell and said, "You can't give me a detention for this, my period just started and it made me late." That was my first experience

33

of being frank with someone about something sexual and watching them squirm. He turned red and excused me—I felt triumphant, but sticky.

The year my period started was the year that a feminist manifesto came out, *The Female Eunuch* by Germaine Greer, which I found on my mother's ironing board one afternoon. The single thing I remember from that book was that she dared readers to taste their own menstrual blood. I had forgotten to do that with all the Tampax reading materials occupying my mind, but I resolved to try it immediately on the next trip to the bathroom. My menses tasted salty, like regular blood; I did not feel any special magic. That was the letdown of my period—I was glad I wasn't frightened, like my mother had been in her experience, but I didn't feel like I'd crossed the threshold of womanhood either. Whenever our school showed those sex ed films to the girls in hygiene class, where the violins soar as young Debbie clutches her sanitary napkin belt to her breast, it was a message to us that this was a tremendous day, a day to feel like a woman instead of a girl. I didn't feel like that, like a woman, until the first time I got pregnant, some sixteen years later.

I have several women friends who can name their children by all the birth control methods that failed. They got pregnant on the pill, taking one each and every day, they got pregnant with an IUD firmly lodged in their uterus, and they got pregnant using every barrier method on the market. Of course, as the missionaries like to point out, you can't get pregnant if you don't have sex, but it is a very human practice that is hard to avoid, even for the chastity crowd. I did not get pregnant my first time by birth control failure. I've used all the methods, and luckily have done well with them all. No, I got pregnant by sheer surprise, by the novelty of it all. I got pregnant because I was a lesbian throwing a tantrum and I was not prepared to be with a man. After spending so many years sleeping with women, it really seemed fantastic to me to connect reproduction with sex—

34

AS IF! I fucked a handsome man that fateful night as if I was in a dream; there was Susie Super-Ego talking on the outside, saying, "What are you doing! You fool, do you think there is some lavender parachute that is going to protect you?" Then there was my body lying there, and responding to this man, and when he released inside me, when I felt the cum on my thighs, it was like, "Well, I'll be damned."

Everyone got very angry at me for being pregnant. My girlfriend, who had lived with me for six years, was livid. The man who knocked me up didn't want to speak to me. My friends thought I had lost my mind: How could I, a sex educator, get myself pregnant like this? It was pathetic. I had never thought of myself as a mother, and my morning sickness was just a physical reminder of how out of control I felt in general. I made plans to get an abortion. I never thought of carrying the baby to term. I had no explanations, I felt very sorry for myself, and I bought myself a giant stuffed bear at the flea market so I could hold on to something that didn't open its mouth and say, "How could you do this?" I didn't feel like a mommy then. I felt like a little girl.

I was relieved after my abortion. My body belonged to me again and I felt intact. I went to the toilet when I returned home, and I was bleeding a little—that was expected—as I cleaned myself up, and I had the feeling I had missed so long ago in seventh grade: I was a woman. I WOULD have a baby, I COULD have a baby if I wanted to—just the breath of that thought escaped me and made me feel very happy. I could picture myself as Mom, for just a second; it was as if my hormones took me by the hand and said, "There, there, now you know."

Every woman's pregnancy is different. There are women who go for months and say they don't feel a thing. But in my case, when I am pregnant, I feel my body nesting for someone else right away. It's rather extraordinary to give your womb, the ultimate host, to another, to give over every function and disposition of your body to feeding and nurturing that new life. When I was pregnant with my daughter Aretha, a year after the abortion, I adored that feeling, because I so looked forward to her birth. I comprehended the true meaning of sacrifice, something I'd been preached to about ad nauseam in Catholic school for years. Carrying a child made it obvious to me: sacrifice is giving yourself up, giving up anything and everything you might care about for another's benefit, and doing so with love, so that even as you feel the loss of what you gave up, you feel it without resentment, without bitterness. It's not something you can make yourself do. "Making oneself" is the opposite of sacrifice, which is really the essence of being a parent, and of mothering in particular. Sacrifice is feminine—it is the liberating and soul-fulfilling aspect of masochism—and it is very rare, because it cannot be captured or ordered on demand.

Having sex to make babies on purpose is thrilling; I can't think of anybody who's done it who didn't feel ecstatic about it. It doesn't even matter whether it's conventional intercourse or not—I've been on the delivery end of a turkey baster, and believe me our cheeks were just as pink, our hopes were just as high. What's so devastating to women is when all our sexuality that isn't about making babies is called into question, given names like "destructive, promiscuous, irresponsible, leading to nothing." My queer delusion when I first got knocked up—"What does sex have to do with making babies?"—was preeminently silly in a practical sense, but very profound in its sexual spirit.

When lovers have sex that doesn't result in pregnancy, it becomes radiantly apparent what OTHER lasting results come from sex: intimacy, self-enlightenment, a source of strength and tenderness and imagination that really can't be uncovered in any other way. One reason I have a rotten time arguing with right-to-lifers is that women who would claim that sex is for making babies have either never experienced a sexual "moment" for themselves, like what I've described above, or perhaps they did and it scared the dickens out of them, because they didn't know what it was or what it could do to them.

In any case, the antiabortion activists project the idea that sex is about babies, about "unborn and innocent children"; and by posing on the stage of innocence and helplessness, they obscure the real issue of abortion rights, which is women's sexuality. How do I know that this is the underlying issue, stopping women from controlling their own sexuality? It's not lying very low, that's how.

If limiting abortion were REALLY about children, then we would have a radically different world than the one we see around us today. If we really felt that children were the focal point of human life, it would not be enough to conceive them. Children would be greeted with the utmost concern and generosity by not only their blood family but by the whole community. The child's education and welfare would be the foundation of social institutions. Choosing to carry a child would be cherished, as much as birth control and abortion would be honored—if the point of giving life was to give a lifetime.

Abortion is nothing less than triage; it is preserving the right to survive for those who have a decent chance of making it. In the hospital setting, that means choosing those who have the most serious needs with the best chance of recovery, and in birth it means choosing children who are wanted, who have the love and nurturing waiting for them that they need to be good parents themselves someday. That's not always an easy thing to judge, but in our current reproductive wars, the mother and child's self-interest are not even the key witnesses.

Now if limiting abortion were about controlling male sexuality, that would be a very funny scene. The way it is now, women are ultimately responsible for saying NO, for pushing that sperm away. Some men will be gallant, some responsible, some fearful, but since none of them—not one—will ever play host to a life growing in his body, they have the PHYSICAL opportunity to literally walk away. They aren't CARRYING the baby: it's as simple as that. Nine months is a long time. Labor is UNFATHOMABLE to men: they will never feel a person COME OUT OF THEM.

If society felt that men were the bottom line in pregnancy prevention, there would be some pretty draconian methods to keep their seed at bay. As the famous seventies pro-choice poster said, "If men got pregnant, abortion would be a sacrament." I guess there'd be a lottery for men who didn't have to get a vasectomy. There would be ruthless punishments for men who caused unauthorized pregnancies. Such a scheme seems too aberrant to continue elaborating.

Yet it isn't considered despicable to plot such a scheme for women's sexuality. The right-to-lifers think that if a woman is pregnant, it doesn't matter if she isn't prepared to be a mom, it doesn't matter what happens to her other children, it doesn't matter if the child is UNWANTED, because they prize their sense of property and morality above all else—and they call their sensibility "innocence." It is not innocent to turn a woman into a puppet, but it is extraordinarily powerful.

The innocence the moralists picture, the cherub angels under God the heavenly father—what kind of mad fantasy are they protecting about their own lives? Some people who want to stop abortions are outright women-haters, you can see it in their righteous gaze: hating women for not living with them, choosing them. Their female counterparts are the sister-punishers, the enforcers in skirts who aren't going to let other women have a life if they can't have one. Other patsies in the God squad are the winsome heartbreakers; they look at you like a wounded animal and ask how you would feel if you had never been born, if *you* had been aborted. That's an easy one—I wouldn't be feeling anything, I wouldn't be taking it personally, because I, in all my fabulous feelingness, would not EXIST! Thank goodness I'm not selfish enough to dream up this crap.

The women's movement has been erratic in its success in protecting abortion rights. I first became sexual in the 1970s, and I could have gone to a pro-choice demonstration every week if I wanted to. Sexual self-determination and abortion accessibility were building blocks of feminist activism. The issue as a cornerstone has never changed, but the activism has. It's something we vote about, it's a personal decision we still agonize about; but it's not something women are out in the streets confronting the hysterics about on a persistent basis. No, the pro-choice movement has been very white-collar and mainstream in recent years, while the street tactics have been almost entirely taken over by the right-to-lifers. That's because abortion, the issue on the streets, has become the domain of so much White Trash. It's those nutty White church groups who don't have an anchor on the middle-class achievement scale, taking their sense of alienation to the clinic picket lines, following the bidding of politicians and religious leaders who wouldn't let them touch the hem of their skirts in normal circumstances.

Antiabortion activism is the most venal of class contradictions. The well-to-do leaders are political opportunists who don't hesitate to hide and get rid of unwanted pregnancies in their own families. Their poor and working-class troops don't have all the same resources and opportunities, but they'll try to ape the denial as best they can. How do I know all this? Because without knowing the famous characters of today's headlines, I know their predecessors. I went to school with middle-class girls from right-to-life families, and when they got knocked up, they often could barely admit it. Maybe it was a dirty towel, maybe it would go away. But THEY went away: some went for a week, some for several months, and when they came back, it was as if NOTHING had happened at all. Far more grotesque than their abortion or adoption was the deceit that they were not sexual, that there was no life inside them.

Here's what women really know about abortion: you can get one if you have the money to get to the right doctor and pay for it.

Middle-class parents who are antiabortion refuse to let an unplanned pregnancy damage them socially. Being "pro-life" is not about babies, it's about controlling your daughter! The other side of abortion, "forced sterilization," is prima-facie evidence for this. Women make sexual decisions—in opposition to their parents' wishes, their lovers' wishes, their neighbors' wishes—and these are the women who have their wombs countermanded if they don't have the education and hard cash to have their own way.

Because we decriminalized abortion in this country so powerfully in the past decades, the class divisions between the empowered and the unempowered have not been so vicious. It has been possible for a working-class woman to get an abortion, or have a child, in her own community without destroying herself in the process. When women don't worry—"Where will I go, how will I be able to afford it?"—when they refuse to keep their pregnancy a secret, when shame isn't the motivating factor in their sexuality, then the substantial issues in a woman's life are able to take precedence: she can consider motherhood in terms of mothering, instead of desperation and the consequences of sin.

When I see our legislators passing restrictions on abortion, never worrying about the women in their own families—when I see the righteousness in the eyes of the clan who think killing the abortion doctor is a blow for freedom—then I tremble both at their arrogance and at the complacency that greets them. We don't have political leaders brave enough to get up and say that abortion is about controlling women and keeping second-class citizens down on the farm. That's pathetic. Instead, we have armies of walking wounded, the unloved, unwanted, unmothered, unfathered—and then we have our elected leaders going around thinking they can make a public policy decision based on this festering ignorance and suffering. They are the mercenaries who say it costs them too much politically to defend abortion. They ask the pro-abortion women, "Who are you to play God, to decide who is good enough or ready to bear children?"

When women's liberation and sexual dignity are your goals, then such false accusations and debates collapse. Women must be free to use everything in medicine, technology, education, and imagination to control their amazing capacity to create, and that independence is what makes life worth caring about.

The second time I had an abortion, I was a mother. In those days, my daughter was four years old and would regularly come into my bedroom in the morning and say, "I want you to make me a baby sister . . . NOW!"

I said, "What would you do if the baby was crying?" and Aretha said, "I'd give it some milk." "And what if the baby was still crying?" I asked.

"Then she would have to take a nap," she said firmly.

I laughed, "What if she didn't want to take a nap?"

"Then she would get a big spanking!" Aretha said, gleefully this time.

Some big sister. I remember the times when I couldn't figure out how to make her stop crying, and I hadn't slept for so long that I thought I would slap her if I didn't remove myself from the scene. I put her, yelling, in her crib and went outside holding a blanket over my ears, crying and reciting some sort of Dr. Spock gibberish to myself. Those times were so hard. I had no clue how I was supposed to keep a full-time job and raise my kid at the same time. I didn't know my body would fail me or how sick I'd get. I've never been so angry and tired. When things got a little better, when my financial and child-care fortunes improved, it was such a revelation to be there for her without feeling like it was a war between us, to have energy for two instead of one and a half.

I guess Aretha's constant demands for a big baby doll made a beeline to my uterus, because I did get pregnant, and this time, when I scheduled the abortion, it was because I knew exactly what it meant to be a mom, what sacrifice and satisfaction is all about as a parent. I'm not raped, or retarded, or unfit to have a child. I simply don't want to threaten the family I live in now. I do wish I were younger, sometimes, or richer, when I feel that wistful baby desire, it is always hemmed in by my closely stitched reality. I like raising children, and my relationships with my extended family's children are precious to me. But I don't want to be the vessel again. Will a group of men with a piece of paper and a gavel in their hands decide whether I can get another abortion?—men who came OUT of us women, but will never deliver or suckle another human being in all their lives? These sons of mothers couldn't stay in labor, or nurture an infant, for a single hour. What are they doing in our lives?

Plagues,
Panics,
and
General
Pandemonium

♀ ♂ ♀ ♂ ♀ ♂ ♀ ♂

Cooties

WE ARE NOW APPROACHING the decline of the AIDS panic. The panic is not anything like the AIDS epidemic itself, which is unfolding as we speak. An AIDS panic is an entirely different creature from the disease.

It seems so long ago now, but when AIDS first came on the scene, people were apoplectic about French kissing. Nowadays, people are dismissing the relative risks of performing fellatio. When someone discovers they are HIV positive, their funeral is not planned on the spot anymore, as we expect them to live many years. Magic Johnson returning to the court—five years after he retired, with the announcement of his HIV infection—is the perfect example of how a panic that swept a sporting field has subsided in favor of showcasing one man's considerable talent and strength. Also, there are now all sorts of famous people who aren't gay but have AIDS, and the notion that the virus is some kind of special punishment for sexual orientation is receding.

The large umbrella of the AIDS panic has broken into many smaller, but no less fearful, panic-ettes. The belief that AIDS is a conspiracy against minorities, for example—black, Latin, Native American, queer—is on the upswing. Looking at the political conditions

45

for racial minorities, or the xenophobic backlash against immigrants, it's no wonder that people who live in a ghetto of racism and/or sexual intolerance have to think twice about the virus's origins.

The other mini-panic that AIDS has spawned is the idea of retribution against sexual excess. AIDS is, mysteriously, considered the disease for two classes of people on the opposite ends of the spectrum: the little innocent children infected by a bad blood transfer— or the sex maniacs. You either get it because you fucked your way into it, or you are the unsuspecting victim of the sex maniacs' irresponsibility. AIDS is a supersexy medical panic—the hype is that you don't get it from having a normal, one- or two-digit sex history. You have to have hundreds of partners, an erotic cast of thousands.

The AIDS panic of promiscuity reflects our traditional fears of sexual gluttony, and a sense that no one can draw the definitive line of what is TOO FAR. We're uneasy watching our boundaries being erased and replaced like a menu instead of a tablet of commandments. Furthermore, when our standards change at home, they don't necessarily get reflected in our institutions. The women's liberation movement, and sexual liberation, have traveled light-years to revolutionize people's intimate boundaries; yet they are strangely unreflected in our laws, or our formal politics.

You can't pick up this fact from our broader cultural take on the plague. My lover, Jon, who is magnetically attracted to bad movies, recently rented the 1995 video *Outbreak,* a movie that still rides the popularity wave of VIRUS HORROR which characterizes every post-AIDS American household today. The movie does a pretty decent job of stirring up any dormant germophobia anyone may have: our next-door neighbors came over and started sneezing halfway through the movie, and the rest of us screamed "Quarantine!" and rolled them up in a blanket.

But *Outbreak* hasn't gotten its hooks in me—the real thing is much more unnerving. It nauseates me just to hear a one-minute news item on the radio that twenty-seven more people died of Ebola virus in Zaire in the past week—the virus that apparently liquefies your insides in a matter of hours, exploding your blood through your eyeballs.

Yeah, *Outbreak* qualifies as a bad movie first and foremost because it isn't scary enough, and, more important, because it has such a super-duper happy ending. Just when beautiful actress Renee Russo is about to die, with what looks like a mild case of acne on her face, Dustin Hoffman finds the bad monkey who started the whole mess, and saves her!

Is this movie actually trying to imply that if someone with Dustin Hoffman's pluck had found the right monkey in the nick of time, we could have stopped AIDS? "What kind of a virus is that?" I asked.

"It's a Hollywood virus," said Jon, and he was just too bleeding correct: *Mr. Smith Goes to the Center for Disease Control.*

I fear the viruses. I know I'm just another set of cells to munch up and spit out; and because I recognize that my vulnerability has nothing to do with my sexual preference, or God's wrath, or bad karma, I suppose I feel even more susceptible. Viral contagion doesn't give a damn about politics or religion. It's terrifying to be so smug that you imagine this could never happen to you, to your family; but, like everyone else, I don't dwell on it any more than I imagine a future fatal car accident. It enters my mind most often after I haven't heard from someone in a while, and one of the first things I wonder is, is s/he still alive? Or when I thumb through my phone book looking for something and I think, I really have to get a new phone book, so many of these people are dead. And then I never get rid of the phone book, because somehow throwing it away would be like throwing away the last vestiges of them.

When I was little, one of my elder relatives would complain that every week another one of her peers had passed away, and she was damned if she was going to stick around to be the last, it was so lonely. Now that experience she described is something that can begin in your twenties. Maybe I shouldn't assume that AIDS has touched everyone's life; I just know that it seemed, one year, that everyone I knew was alive and kicking, and then the next year rolled around, and everyone started failing, or checking out, or fighting to the bitter end, accepting death with grace or denying it with insanity. Whatever the method, I became familiar with them all, and in the end a whole lifetime of friends had left me for good. Psychically, all the people who remained alive changed into a bunch of eighty-year-old women, who'd outlived everyone they grew up with and gave birth to.

Still, there are families and pockets of America where AIDS is not oppressive, where the war has not come home. I don't know what it is about the isolation of the mainstream media, but I still see the biggest bozos dominating public discussion about the whys and wherefores of AIDS prevention and STD transmission.

The year I wrote this book, another famous athlete—and there are dozens of them now—the boxer Tommy Morrison, was disclosed as having tested positive for HIV, and immediately was withdrawn from further matches. A sports columnist named Jason Whitlock from the *Kansas City Star* was overcome with alarm and despair over this turn of events and wrote a front-page editorial that was reprinted even in my small-town California newspaper.

Whitlock seemed to believe Tommy's troubles were inevitable because, after all, Tommy had a reputation as a ladies' man, an insatiable girl chaser, well known to the local after-hours crowd. The columnist felt like it was time to talk to our children and tell them that screwing around is not what it means to be a man, to be a grown-up.

What any of this sanctimonious hand-wringing had to do with AIDS is beyond me. Tommy could have fucked thirty women, or ten, or three, but if he was unfortunate enough to have had high-risk sex with one positive woman—particularly if he had sex with this same woman more than once—then he could be infected, and all the monogamy in the world couldn't have saved him after that. Tommy is not sero-positive because he is a slut; he is positive because he was infected in a single sexual or blood-sharing encounter, and nobody really knows anything more than this.

If Tommy had sex with many, many partners, for instance, but habitually used condoms for intercourse—or had other kinds of sex that avoided semen and blood sharing—then he wouldn't have been as safe as a complete celibate, but his risk for HIV would have been minuscule. He would certainly be at lower risk than a man who had fewer partners but chancier sexual behavior.

Maybe we should get this celibacy thing cleared up once and for all. What are the track records of people who have chosen celibacy for their spiritual or professional calling? Priests and superstitious athletes come immediately to mind. Everyone knows that these highly motivated people have slipped up right and left.

Or how about the "scare 'em safe" techniques? These are the choice of everyone who gets their kicks from intimidating teenagers. A theater group from Pittsburgh, the Saltworks Theatre Company, has played three hundred gigs this past year, and now is performing a "No sex is safe sex" drama called *No Safe Place* on public-school stages around the country.

A reporter who saw the show in Middletown, Connecticut, Katherine Ogden, wrote that the young actors in the play mime a game of Russian roulette to show how risky it is to use condoms for protection. One of the hapless characters has sex only twice: the first time, she gets HIV, and the second time she passes it on to someone else. I think the first person who slept with her should have been made a homosexual Martian, but that might have been asking too much.

"Because of me, that person is going to die," says Maureen in her final dying scene. "I regret that. And I regret that I won't get to graduate." Oh, yeah, graduation, the ultimate life experience. But if Maureen joins the Cannabis Club to get wholesale drug relief, starts writing for a militant-positive 'zine like *Diseased Pariah News,* and gets some hip doctors, she'll probably live way past the prom. Maybe she'll even have sex and fall in love with someone else who's positive like her!

My hopes are false. All the actors in the Saltpeter group emphasize Christian values and have made a commitment to abstain from sex until marriage. After reading about their touring schedule, I'd be surprised if they could make it through their three hundred performances without a little hanky-panky—I know what it's like to perform on the road. These people's own grown-up lives are going to make a mockery out of their script's message.

Teenagers are easy to scare because they're anxious about sex to begin with, AIDS or no AIDS. There's nothing that pleases the puritan demagogues more than hearing a bunch of hormone-impaired junior high school students shouting "Pee-uuew! Sex is icky, I'm taking the Chastity Pledge!" Kids are under peer pressure to do a million things, and they will grab at any righteous reason to justify their fears as if it were a tootsie pop.

When I was that age, I was 100 percent sure that everyone in my tenth-grade class had experienced sex except me, and that's why I was at the bottom of the popularity deck. The day after I did have sex with another person for the first time, I walked down the school halls to my locker and all around me, like a trembling skin, I could see them—VIRGINS. Hardly anyone was having sex; they were scared shitless. I couldn't see the obvious when I was trembling as badly as the rest.

As soon as frightened people have an opportunity to have sex that doesn't seem frightening, they will grab it, they will take that chance, and bye-bye go the celibacy vows. It can be because of something as wonderful as a kind lover's guidance, or as sloppy as getting high and not giving a hoot.

People are not going to stop having sex in any kind of significant numbers just because they're scared, or because it's dangerous. I always knew sex was fraught with danger. For one, I would have felt like my life was over if I had gotten pregnant when I was sixteen—I agonized with friends who faced that dilemma. Even without the physical chances of getting more than you bargained for in sexual relations, there were all the psychological hurdles. Physical intimacy could so easily mean falling in love, unbearable longing, a broken heart. Who would put up with all of it if it weren't such a terribly HUMAN thing to do, if the urge to sexually connect wasn't in our souls, our maturity, our fingertips?

To "just say no" is a fine thing for many occasions, not only sexual ones. I wish I could have said no to my mechanic last week, for example. I'm always kicking myself for not having the moxie to tell people my boundaries, ahead of time. But saying "no" is nothing more than crying wolf if the person saying it doesn't know the power of also affirming "yes." It's distinguishing what you DO want, and knowing the advantages of it, that gives the "no's" their currency. People who have a lot of sexual experience and know what they enjoy sexually always give the very best no's. It's almost a pleasure to be on the receiving end of their refusal, because their confidence and goodwill is contagious.

Career celibacy and automated "no" responses are science fiction, as fantastic as an amazing world where people don't eat, or cry, or poop. The appeal of celibacy has always been to transcend human desire, the lower chakras, the elemental and earthy parts of ourselves. Well, too bad, that's the way we were made, and we should take a hint from the other animals around us. You don't see birds starting an antiflying campaign just because the skies aren't so friendly anymore. Sex is not all-consuming; it's just a natural part of our lives that we have often repressed for all its mysteries.

Some people think safer sex advice, condoms, dams, and all the rest are too complicated. It's true that there's a lot of information out there, but I don't know anyone who's sorry that they're informed, or bummed out because they got the latest update. It's not that challenging to learn and internalize matters of interest to your body. The real problem is how sex information is censored and suppressed so that people can't get it in the first place. Furthermore, if safe sex is offered like cod liver oil, it's not going to be swallowed. Safe sex doesn't work without sexual fulfillment—that's why I started to do workshops called "Safe Sex for Sex Maniacs," because I had to do something dramatic to break through the forbidding qualities of so many safety do's and don'ts.

My workshop title had that kind of oxymoronic titillation that would draw a big crowd wherever I went. How can "safer sex" be something that a true sex aficionado would enjoy? Aren't sex maniacs the ones who are responsible for all our troubles? No—people who think, talk, and have sex a lot are the answer to your prayers, because they're the only ones with any experiential information.

The most frustrating thing about safer sex info is these giant fuzzy areas where no one knows the complete answer. When we do hit a gray spot, everyone tends to fall back on their worst fears about, and condemnation of, sex. The most obvious case of this quandary is oral sex. I once had a poignant discussion about oral sex with a support group of HIV-positive women. When asked what they missed most about their postdiagnosis sex, they said, almost to a woman, "Having my pussy licked!" (When asked what they most enjoyed, postdiagnosis, that they never did before in sex, the overwhelming answer was "Vibrators.") Everyone in the group was terribly worried about the risk of cunnilingus passing the virus to their partner, and since no one in HIV research was giving the time of day to women's bodily fluids at that time (the late eighties), it was a big mystery. Women generally feel so insecure and suspicious about their cunts to begin with that having another reason to keep their lips shut seemed the familiar—thus, the safer—thing to do.

I teased them, saying they needed to start the day with a pussy affirmation: "My lips are beautiful, my clitoris is beautiful, I smell like a woman. When I open my legs, the world begins"—something along those lines. We could all have a good laugh, because it's unusual to have those feelings at all, let alone after you've been diagnosed positive.

As it turns out, oral sex research has shown us what is typical of all news about this virus—that it has nothing to do with all our self-loathing insecurities about our bodies. The HIV virus does exist in women's genital fluids, as well as in sperm. But oral/genital transmission is a very poor way for the virus to infect you. It's not the party your virus wants to go to. The more important aspect of oral contact seems to be the character of the mouth, rather than the genitals. Many people have gums that bleed, or a mouth sore, and it's this blood opening that poses the highest risk. That's why today's hottest date tip is: Don't brush your teeth, girls, and for heaven's sake, no FLOSSING! This must drive dentists berserk, because of course if you brush and floss regularly, your gums will be pink and lovely and never bleed—but how many of you can say in all honesty that your dentist is going to give you a blue ribbon on that account?

There are other things to consider about the health of your mouth, since any sores or STD already affecting the vulva or penis also pose a risk factor. But risk factor isn't the same as HIGH risk. Letting people know all the little details puts a lot of discretion in their hands, but it's the only honest way to go. If we persist in being alarmists about oral sex in general, the word gets out that people are doing it, or some variation of it (to swallow or not to swallow—or how quickly to do either—is the question), and surviving quite nicely.

53

What's interesting to me about the oral sex question is that it becomes apparent that we are not embarrassed to show our mouths, open our mouths—we are not doing the veil number, and we aren't stigmatizing people who don't use fluoride! So much damage is done in the name of safe sex education by making people feel shame about their genitals, as if not knowing what you look like and how your sexual cycles function would save your ass. It's just the opposite. Prudery kills.

The key to being as safe as you wanna be is not carrying a list of outdated rules in your pocket: it's listening to your own body, talking frankly with your lovers and friends, and getting the most uncensored facts and research material available. It's realizing that these days your zip code is probably a higher risk factor than your sexual preference, because this disease is demographic, not prejudicial. It means you have to pull your head out of the sand and forget mainstream television, which is spreading a virtual disinformation campaign, and instead look for your local gay paper, or the nearest free-needle IV-drug user center. There you'll find the people who have the most conscientious and practical information. STDs are here to stay—like the weather—and if you want to know where it's raining, you have to tune in.

But what if you're like poor little Rapunzel, all locked up in a turret with no friends to turn to? In that situation, Safer Sex for Sex Maniacs offers alternatives: one is when you're with someone you don't know and there are no condoms in sight, you can simply avoid sharing blood and semen, and let your dirty little mind come up with a different style of orgasm. Safe sex HABITS, the familiarity, won't work if you can't get off—to say anything else is a puritanical joke. The excitement of desire is ultimately what will send you to the moon, including all the "unsafe" fantasies you can dream up. You can envision gallons of sperm from fifty cowboys pumping up your ass, and that's a lovely and completely safe way to get your rocks off.

If only Tommy Morrison had done that, and spanked all his dozens of girlfriends while they sucked and stroked his penis with their sticky eager groupie hands, he would be in the pink today, and that fretful columnist would have to come up with some other drivel to spook his nieces and nephews.

Despite what our culture feels about "excessive" sex, it's clear that we think a lot more is acceptable than we used to. Mere homosexuality has become positively wholesome, if one looks at the role models available to the public today. We have fetishized virginity, but we no longer make a condition out of it for a woman's value. We are not shocked that someone has had, say, ten sexual partners. Sex before marriage is considered sensible, not a sin. We do not condemn lovers because they have oral or anal sex or use a vibrator; and as much as we esteem loyalty and partnership, people are not damning their partners or their friends to everlasting hell for infidelity. The notion of marriages that are in some way erotically open to interpretation is hardly shocking.

Of course, there are "old-fashioned" people defending the old values, but the point is, everyone is in agreement that they're OLD. The biggest lie the old-fashioned people have on their side is that sexuality used to be so different in the good OLD days, when in fact it was only more secretive, and much more restrictive for women and young people. One day, AIDS will be an anachronistic disease, but the panic, the revolution—our transformed respect for life and death and sex—will never be plowed under.

The Medford Incident

MEDFORD, OREGON, DECEMBER 1995: *Roxanne Ellis and Michelle Abdill, a lesbian couple in southern rural Oregon, were murdered by a stranger named Robert James Acremant, who shot them in the back of the head after abducting them in his truck. The couple was well known in their community as realtors and also as activists who campaigned against an antihomosexual proposition on the ballot the previous year.*

I FIRST HEARD ABOUT the Medford murders through a string of e-mail messages that appeared in my computer mailbox. Gay activists across the country were horrified by the savagery of the killings and immediately connected the tragedy to the rise in violent homophobia and antigay politicking. Many observers noted the risks that a lesbian faces in coming out of the closet could include losing her life.

This last conclusion was the first to disturb me; it angered me that people felt these women were killed because they had the courage and presence of mind not to hide their relationship behind closed doors. I think it's an old wives' tale, and a really stale one at that, that people who come out are more vulnerable to victimization than those who lie and conceal and fester. It's people who live in the closet that have a bad smell; they're the first to notice it, too, and it makes them want to cover it up all the more. Their odor attracts bullies, ball-busters, blackmailers, and con artists who recognize a certain similarity.

I think the example of an open lesbian couple selling real estate and being well known in their southern Oregon community—a haven for mavericks, land lovers, and westerners—is just about the best security blanket you could purchase under the circumstances. Their position commanded respect, if not always affection.

As it was, Roxanne and Michelle were not killed because they were activists—their murderer knew nothing of their politics. When the man's history unfolded, it became clear that he didn't shoot them because of their sexual preference. A week earlier, Acremant had blown away his best friend as they took a drive together—just to see how it felt. His discussions with the newspaper revealed someone who was clearly insane. "Lesbians, no, I don't like them, but bisexuals are great," he told the reporter, as if he were being interviewed for a matchmaking service.

After Acremant blabbed his life story to the press, more gay press e-mail and circulars came to my house, this time condemning the media and police for not recognizing this murder as a homophobic "hate crime."

Well, it wasn't. This man no more hated his victims for being dykes than he hated them for being realtors, or for being human beings like his best friend who he'd slaughtered earlier. The real cruelty of this man's state of mind was that he was completely removed from emotions like "hate"; he had no compassion for, or comprehension of, others. He was supremely alienated from his own self.

At this point, I was a little ashamed to realize that I was fuming more at the misfiring knee-jerk gay activists than I was at the psychopath. Was I turning into a contrarian ditto-head? Am I so spoiled by San Francisco that all I can do is curl my lip at whatever queen has her panties in a twist? It was hard to think that I'd become so callous, and I thought about the last time I'd had someone take a swipe at me for being gay.

Since I'm a public figure, I get verbal taunts and critiques all the time, but it took me a little more time to think of the last occasion I actually felt threatened on the street. It was about eight years ago—a drunk man was harassing me and my girlfriend at the bus stop, in broad daylight; she wanted to fight him, and I was trying to drag her away.

We had these "fight or flee" arguments all the time, both of us driven by unarguable impulses. I'm always fearful when the provocateur is bigger and stronger than me. I'm instantly aware that he could hurt us, I want to run run run; and afterward, when I'm far enough away, I start to burn up. I hate him so much, I feel like a helpless child, I fantasize a thousand ways I could humiliate and hurt him. My girlfriend was the opposite: she feels the hate, not the fear, first, and she is not impressed by differences in size. She would say to me, "I know that I will fight to the end, I don't care what happens to me, to them, to anything—and they can feel that—having nothing to lose beats muscles every time."

Later, hours after the incident, she would feel frightened, she would wish that she could have turned the other cheek, she would feel like she had lost something, whether it was a tooth or a sense of faith.

I've been attacked by strangers in public places for being a "fucking dyke" a handful of times, and it has always scared the pants off of me. It has also felt the same as when I was attacked alone on the street, *without* being tagged as a dyke, just as a girl with a purse and a pussy. In every case, the motive was supposedly robbery, but it was always sexualized in a proprietary sort of way; like it wasn't enough to get my cash or my rings, I had to worship the perp's dick, too. It was sexy for them, sadistic and sexy, the adrenaline rush of cornering me, intimidating me with a weapon, my body compliant and afraid. When the bastard started touching me, it didn't feel like my body anymore to me, I'd be so frozen up; and sure enough, my body became their lifeless toy, it was *their* tits to pinch, not mine, their cunt lips to open, their tongue in what used to be my mouth.

Afterward, it's just like the rape center pamphlets say: You can't wash the son of a bitch off, you feel like sitting under a boiling hot tsunami, getting out the Brillo pads. You want to crawl out of that skin that he handled and get yourself a new bag.

A typical attack on a dyke, on any woman, is one in which she is made into property, his brand/cock gets placed on her. If she defies him, if she fights back, or does her own thing, if she acts like she doesn't belong to him or anybody else, then it's going to get even uglier. The Medford killer was atypical in this way; his crime was not one of sexual claim. Men who get violent with lesbians in extreme ways tend to be men who used to be married to the "lesbian" in question; it's not even what their ex's orientation really is, but the idea that she has rejected him sexually and his claim upon her is what incites his rage.

When men go fag-bashing, on the other hand, it is not about property and sexual control. It is about fear of femininity: a hot flash that goes through a man when he sees another man who makes him feel—if only for a second—like a girl. For the queer-beater there is NOTHING worse than feeling like a woman, that soft mouth, those pretty hands—you have to squish it. It's sexual, not in the sense of getting a hard-on like it is with bullying women, but sexual in the asking of the question, "I'm a MAN, what the fuck are you?" And when that sentiment is set in a group, the fag-basher is saying something much more important to his friends—his voyeurs or fellow participants—than he is to his victim.

It's a pretty ugly portrait of men, isn't it? This is why a book like *Woman Hating* by Andrea Dworkin has such appeal based on the title alone. You have men hurting women because they've got to be under men's thumbs—and it's made sexy that way, too. Or you've got men hurting men because every man can't be a man in his own way—there have to be the femmes, the weak ones, and they have to be sacrificed so someone else can be a REAL man. Like there's not enough BOY in the world to go around. It's a pretty radical response to femininity, either way: Feeling like women are not equal in their humanity or free to be as independent as men (so you can treat them like dogs), or treating men "who act like women" as if they shouldn't be allowed to live, like it's the lowest they can go, and they have to be put out of that misery.

Women get violent—who doesn't know that?—but when you think about it, women don't attack men from the point of view of being superior, they attack from the second-class citizen's point of view. Women don't pull out the superior shit except when they beat their children; it's the classic dogpile. And when women strike out against other women, it's not in response to a fight over identity. Who ever heard of a woman beating another woman up because her hair was too short, or because she wouldn't wear a nice dress? Women are likely to turn on themselves for not being feminine enough, beautiful enough, thin enough, and they can be snobs about other women failing to meet these same standards. But this is not why they pull a gun or throw a pot of boiling water at someone. Women attack other women like a couple of satellites thrown into competition, fighting for proximity to the sun—but when they fight men, they face down the sun. People often laugh at women fighting: it's so absurd, it's a sex fantasy, it's entertainment. There's something silly about it. Watching people who don't have power go at it with each other is, truly, an amusement to the onlooker, and either a calculation or a humiliation to the participants. When women want to really punish another member of their sex, they drag a man into it.

How many women have done what I did the other day? I jokingly call it "Making Sexism Work for You." I had just been treated like a piece of shit at the dry cleaners, of all places, trying to get some pillowcases repaired. It was so bizarre; the dry cleaners is usually such an emotionless place, that when the seamstress got unexpectedly nasty, I withdrew into deferential timidity. I was ashamed of my Bambi-ness when I got home, and thought about my next move. I MUST liberate my pillowcases from the Pillow Bitch, I vowed. I have to get my property and my money back. I said to my boyfriend, "Yeah, I know this is a strange favor, but I want you to come with me to the Pillow Bitch and just stand there, don't wear a dress, just display your evident manhood and let's see what happens."

Oh, yes, my instincts were right; Pillow Bitch turned into Pillow Pouter, still sulking but not showing her claws. Instead of thanking Jon, or congratulating myself for my strategy, I felt more outraged than ever—the backlash of "Making Sexism Work for You"—all the more reason to use it only in pillowcase fiascos and not more important matters. If a man standing next to me is my safety net, how dependent does that make me feel? I'd feel more on my own two feet with a big dog.

Lesbians can't use heterosexual partnerships as a self-defense program. It's no wonder they were the instigators of the women's self-defense and martial arts projects that call on women to throw their own weight around to its greatest effect. Yet these programs, and all the well-equipped women they've turned out, were no defense against the strangely passionless work of the Medford killer. He was neither a common street criminal nor an aggressive family member. But he is not representative of a wave of violence against lesbians. There is no wave—it's the same as it ever was—and moreover, this isn't how lesbians are typically bullied and attacked. There are nut cases out there, but they are not the face of institutional prejudice, religious righteousness, or unrelenting discrimination. Those are nuts of a different color.

No, lesbians are attacked the way all women are attacked—for their dispute with some man's property rights, which he may interpret as his "dignity." A man who feels that women are property is sure to be offended when they act as equals and competitors. Now most men wouldn't say they think a woman is the same as a piece of real estate—but they may have walked over so many women that they don't appreciate the difference anymore between the ground and their female support system. They notice pretty fast when the ground slips out from under them, though. That's the first opportunity for a violent reaction—and that's where women, be they dykes, outlaws, or a more self-possessed generation, are drawing the line.

How Safe Is Your Daughter?

IN MY MIND, IT started with the milk cartons. One day, the breakfast bowl of cereal was no longer accompanied by a back-of-the-box advertisement for secret decoder rings or action-toy figurines. Instead, the box art that held my early-morning attention was the back of the milk container, where a little face peered out at me, a missing child, with her name listed urgently alongside a set of statistics about her age, hair color, and the time she was last seen.

Next week, next breakfast, there was another face. It was heartbreaking and anxiety provoking all at once—the notion that every week, every gallon, there would be another missing kid. Who was stealing the children?

Kidnapping was clearly the threat of these announcements. The implication of the "Missing" headline was that some despicable monster had made off with these children, and now their parents' only hope was that one of us, one of the decent people at the breakfast table, would spot young Timmy or curly-haired Sandy and get on the line to 1-800-MIS-SING on the double.

Why would someone want to steal a child? Our imaginations lead us to envision a sexual, sadistic purpose. Evil has to come to mind—for there is simply no "innocent" reason to take children from their home.

The alarm of the "Missing Milk Carton Kids" was so dynamic, so successful in its titillation of American fears, that while the campaign was still in its infancy, reporters and social workers and cynics of all types started to question its assumptions. Were these children really missing? Or were they the ransom notes of a child custody fight? Or runaways with urgent agendas of their own?

As sex panics go, the milk carton campaign was investigated rather early, and the resulting revelations yielded depressing, if not exactly evil, results. Sexual sadists were not kidnapping children in record numbers—that was revelation number one. But children *were* in turmoil at home in ways that reflected ugly gaps between both genders and generations.

For starters, outlaw child custody battles have become a regular business, in which parents "kidnap" the kids back and forth from each other like jewelry, as much to strike blows against their estranged mates as to protect the child's interests. Courts, social workers, and extended family members are often faced with parental tugs-of-war which, more than anything, raise the question, Where does a parent's ego end and a child's life begin?

Furthermore, teenagers were leaving their families, intact or not, of their own accord, looking for a way out: "Yes, I've been abducted, and I'm never coming home." If another adult didn't offer these young adults an escape, they were following the tribe—other teenagers offering a family apart from the birth family. Not all those kids were abandoning a physically abusive situation; some had just realized their families could no longer support them, emotionally or financially. In a sense, the parents were the ones who ran away—or were in a state of parental catatonia.

Finally, you have the blessedly emancipated: teenagers who are living in their own households, of whatever sort, with the affection and support, on some level, of their birth parents. I was one of those. I dropped out of high school my second year, got my own apartment, and my father not only bought me an old stove and refrigerator but he also carried them up two flights of stairs to install them in my very own roach-infested kitchen. Whenever I think of my father groaning under the weight of that refrigerator, I remember how I thought my heart would burst with love for him. I don't know why he didn't insist that I should be kept on a short leash, but his support—installing the stove and then getting out of the way—made the difference between my being an emancipated minor or a runaway teenager.

Of course, not every milk carton kid can be explained away by the alternative circumstances I've laid out. The case of even one child who has been dragged off by a crazy stranger is a horror of unfathomable depths. Those stories are what galvanize the public consciousness. We make monsters out of a couple of deviant characters, but if we had to match every "missing" kid's face to the primary adult in their lives, we wouldn't be looking at a lineup of outsider degenerates—we'd be facing ourselves and our own family histories. We can't act as if all the "decent" people are all on one side of the breakfast table and the inhuman creepsters are on the other. Their indifference or cruelty to—or exploitation of—their kids makes us blanch, but don't call them "unnatural." Grown-ups have been fucking kids and fucking them over, creating them and protecting them and letting go of them, treating them like property, loving them badly and loving them inadequately and loving them mindlessly—FOREVER. If we really wanted to change the face of abandonment and abuse, we'd give more respect and power to children than we do to fetuses. And I don't mean giving your child a lollipop every time he screams for one. What I have in mind is more like a revolution.

It's very difficult to imagine a revolution of sons and daughters. The context around me is the story of Oedipus's revenge, which is usually merged with the fashion of blaming everything that's new and shiny around us. I am accustomed to viewing child-nappings and missing victims from our late twentieth-century bogeyman perspective.

When a child-robber, the culprit, is found, I'm not at all surprised to hear that he has a porno collection in his closet, for example. It bothers me, but I'm not surprised, since so many nonculprits have porno collections as well. I run to my own soapbox to reassure all who will listen that porno doesn't lead to sexual crimes any more than the fact that the offender also eats mashed potatoes.

But then other habits of the porn deviant come to light, and there are even more objects that evoke our suspicion and I-told-you-so's: The perpetrator ate . . . junk food. He frequented . . . gay bars. He spent a lot of time in . . . AOL chat rooms. In his glove compartment were found traces of . . . drugs. Sound familiar?

Now there must be a zillion sociable gay men who eat Doritos, smoke marijuana, and use a computer, who would no sooner hurt a fly than harm a child. But we tend to magnify these aspects of people's modern lives when someone is accused of something sordid and kinky. We look for the things that appeal to the senses, our notions of vice, as well as our dread of new technology that presumably brings those same vices ever closer to our fingertips.

Technology and modern culture are the top reasons for today's sex panics: the Internet pedophile scares, the violent movies and rap music that are rumored to turn our youth into soulless nihilists, the relatively easy availability of sex toys and tattoos and black leather G-strings. Yet these bright and stinging targets have as ephemeral a connection to sex crimes as the tabloids they're written up in.

Let's take a nostalgic look back at three sex crimes against children that roused our entire country's outrage:

> ON NOVEMBER 14, . . . Linda Joyce Glucoft, aged six years, was sexually assaulted by an elderly relative of the friend she had gone to visit in her Los Angeles neighborhood. When she cried out, her assailant, a retired baker who the police had already charged in another child molestation case, choked her with a necktie, stabbed her with an ice pick, and bludgeoned her with an ax, then buried her body in a nearby rubbish heap.

Only a few days later, a drunken farm laborer assaulted and murdered a seventeen-month-old baby girl outside a dance hall in a small town near Fresno. That same week, the Idaho police found the body of seven-year-old Glenda Brisbois, who had last been seen entering a dark blue sedan near her home; she had been murdered by a powerful assailant who had heaved her body fifteen feet into an irrigation canal.

The gruesome details of these murders and of the hunt for their perpetrators were telegraphed to homes throughout the country by the nation's press. According to police statistics, such assaults were proportionately no more common than in previous years, but . . . these three murders epitomized to many Americans the heightened dangers that seemed to face women and children. . . . Many regarded them not as isolated tragedies but as horrifying confirmation that a plague of "sex crime" threatened their families.

If the details of these crimes are fresh in your mind, then you must be old enough to be my mother. These murders happened in 1949, nearly half a century ago, and are related here as a history lesson from George Chauncey Jr.'s article, "The Postwar Sex Crime Panic" *(True Stories from the American Past)*. Obviously, given the time frame, there was no fast food, dope, rap music, or MTV to pin the blame on. No porn videos, or even *Playboy* magazine. People did not say *fuck* in *The New Yorker*.

Nevertheless, these terrible deaths spurred parents and legislators into a first-class sex panic, the first real doozy after the war. How could these things happen in America? How could we fight enemies abroad and then face this in our neighborhoods? This wasn't the face of communism or fascism; it was something much more frightening, a group of predators destroying the very littlest, the most innocent. By our society's beliefs, drawn from our understanding of man's relationship to God and each other, the perpetrators who committed these acts must have thought about them beforehand, and the reason they thought about them was because the devil was in their minds, they had been corrupted by something that was not in God's plan.

God and country and righteousness seemed to reach their apex after the sex crimes of 1949, when J. Edgar Hoover published an article in *American Magazine* called "How Safe Is Your Daughter?" A barrage of subsequent articles on sex crime seemed to confirm that she wasn't safe at all.

Alongside the FBI director's cautionary tale, a poster with the same headline was produced featuring three girls of different grade-school ages cringing and fleeing from a giant wart-covered hand hovering in the air over them. Conjuring up every parent's greatest fear—that some harm might come to his or her child—this image urged support for the policing of a wide range of sexual nonconformists. The picture's giant hand also suggested the period's sci-fi horror films, which depicted the threats posed to America by alien ways of life; the implication was that every "sex deviant" was equally alien to traditional American values.

The whole smell of "How Safe Is Your Daughter?" was that of evil strangers, motivated by "deviant" impulses—people who looked like they didn't belong in "our neighborhood," with all the jingoistic and conformist attitudes that implies. The group that took the brunt of society's paranoia was gay men, adult homosexuals who were just beginning to develop a real counterculture after the war—but who were in no way out of the closet. Hoover's maniacal persecution of gay people belied his own forty-four-year gay relationship and ironically revealed all of America's consciousness, terrified and simultaneously titillated by the crumbling status quo.

The Stonewall Riots were light-years away in the fifties; as in many apathetic eras, people were dieting, not rioting. Homosexuals were thought of as opportunistic pedophiles for all occasions who would just as soon violate a little girl as a little boy. Hoover's call to arms, which pinpointed "daughters" as the likely victims (the "help-less female" mindset), was also a covert call to attack "abnormal" queers—understood to be effeminate men. A straight-line extrapolation of that deviant paranoia would go something like this: Protect your daughters by rooting out femininity in grown men!

Whatever the inhumanities forced on disposable children of the postwar years—or the similarly treated children of today—the ghosts and lessons have been drowned out by the cry of "Hunt Down the Pervert"—the pervert being anyone who doesn't fit the gender-role straitjacket.

Sex panics always seem to be a wake-up call for social change. Rather than looking at one suffering, one victim, we have the opportunity to understand what *everyone* is clenching their fists over. Where is the crystal ball that tells us what today's sexual panics mean?

Well, for one thing, you have to work your kinky mojo just a little bit harder today to qualify as a social undesirable. You can't just be GAY—you have to be one of those blatant queers who wants to get married in Central Park and then kiss in front of everyone with your leather chaps and your tattooed wedding vows televised live on the Internet.

Actually, I don't think people feel their children—that is, THEIR OWN innocence, THEIR OWN sexual anxiety—are so much threatened by queer OPENNESS as by the specter of the weird loner, the person holed up in the suburbs or out in the country somewhere, making up his own existence and using other people's bodies to help him achieve his little catharsis. From the Unabomber to Ted Bundy to Jeffrey Dahmer (even though not all these men were "sex" criminals) the public is aware, as the FBI profiles suggest, that these guys had relationship problems. They couldn't connect to guys OR gals, and their desire to have total control over everything means they never suffered the pains of compassion or empathy—or, for that matter, mature lust.

It's truly a relief that the public sensibility of what makes people dangerous is not that they're effeminate but that they are dangerous because they are ALIENATED. That's quite a switch. The deviant of the late twentieth century is the man who doesn't know how to give or receive love. This discovery has the potential to horrify us even more than deeds, because deep inside we think, my God, it's just the end product of our civilization, the dumping ground for the price of progress. What have we gained materially that was worth so many souls?

When I was a teen in the seventies, I had a couple of episodes when strange men were frightening or threatening me in a sexual way. One of them was a perfect candidate for the sex scares of the time (businessman who picks up hitchhikers from the beach), and the other positioned himself in the bosom of normality (an undergrad studying in the public library). As it turned out, the one who harassed, stalked, and threatened me for months was the guy who asked to borrow my pencil at the library. The man who exposed his penis to my girlfriend and me while he drove us down Sunset Boulevard got frightened and pulled over to let us out of the car the moment we ordered him to. I never saw him again. The man in the library was handsome and chatty. The man in the car was ugly and soundless; the only thing they had in common was that they preyed on someone, a young woman, who they felt was appealingly unthreatening.

The lesson I took from these episodes at the time was that I had gotten in trouble at the library because I had been deferential and polite, whereas my girlfriend in the car had countermanded that situation by giving the driver a direct order to pull over. She looked like she'd as soon pistol-whip him as speak to him. I thought if I cultivated that look of hers, I'd be much better prepared for the world.

It's hard to prepare when you are predisposed and lovingly trained to be a girly-girl. When I took my first self-defense class, I was amazed to see a sixty-year-old classmate of mine show off what she was made of by swinging her purse like a witch's broom at a pretend assailant. Meanwhile, my first instinct when attacked was to mentally leave my body and become effectively paralyzed. My senior classmate was ready to FIGHT; I wasn't, and it was partly because I was unwilling to be territorial, to control the situation, to take over. In other words, to defend yourself against pricks, you have to act a little more like them. I didn't like that lesson, but I couldn't see any alternative except avoidance.

In my television guide, I see that this week's movie is about a mother and her child who are stalked, terrorized, and almost rubbed out by a man who's tracing their every move on the Internet. The villain looks just like the cute guy who started researching me in the library. In the TV guide, the behind-the-scenes article interviews the lead actress who supposedly refused the first script because it was just another helpless female tied to the tracks, screaming and freaking every time Snidely Whiplash made another modem step in her direction.

"I didn't just want to be the typical female role, where I would only REACT," said the star.

Yes, but if she really took charge, she would ruin the panic, ruin the empathy. Someone's got to be the girl and scream her head off, so we know we're still alive! And some courageous girl, "The Final Girl," as film theorist Carol Clover calls her, has got to be the one who holds up a bright white shield and faces the monster down.

This is today's feminist twist to the sex-panic monster: instead of your husband or J. Edgar Hoover saving you, all the men in the story become consumed in the slime, and only the original symbol of innocence can save herself. Whole crowds of men these days are infuriated by the notion that everything bad is placed at men's feet, the fleet of injustices blamed upon the nearly extinct white male, but the annoying part of their complaint is that THEY created it. Men think the worst of men; they can't be their own heroes anymore, especially when they believe that their sexual impulses can't be controlled. As long as they think they are beasts who can only be controlled by a woman's gentle hand, they are prisoners of gender.

I predict that Sex Panics of the future will continue to demonize male sexuality and flirt with the ideas of women's domination—or rather of femme domination, a sort of Amazon class of dykes, virgins, mothers, and drag queens. Meanwhile, the "missing" children are better described as "angry" and impatient—sick of adults appropriating their lives to feed their own neuroses. The youth culture knows there's a gender revolution going on, and they design their bodies and their tribe to express it. They will continue to travel in packs to defend themselves, and don't try to dissuade them by preaching against "gangs"—they know that's just a bourgeois way of dissing someone else's family.

America will boomerang from Fear of a Black Planet, a Youth Planet, and a Genderfuck Planet to the opposite horror: that of a lone man with a big gun—the older, white, had-all-the-opportunities guy who now comes equipped with a bomb, no dates, and a pathologically self-centered attitude. Oh, we'll wish he'd only been in the Crips! If only he'd been a drag queen, if only he'd just pierced his dick and gotten high on dope! Any of those would be preferable, a million times more humane. We could understand a counterculture, but what are we supposed to do with a counterhuman? We can't stand to look at the cult of alienated masculinity and wonder how we got there.

Born-Again Virgin

WHAT IS UP WITH sex lives of the people who love to say NO? Does the God Squad ever entertain impure thoughts? And if they do, how does it affect their politics?

The irony of questioning a conservative's sex life is that so many people think it's too damn rude to ask, while the crusading right wing makes it a point of principle to ask about everyone else's sex lives. Are you now or have you ever been a homosexual? Do you practice sodomy in the privacy of your own home? How old were you when you first had sex? How many people have you slept with? Which ones did you only lust after? Did you practice chastity as a teenager? Do you touch yourself in forbidden places? Why don't you have any children?

Jesus, Mary, and Joseph—if we put fundamentalist candidates on a panel and made them answer all these SAME questions they ask the sinning American public, how many would answer truthfully, if at all? I suppose the smartest of them would say, "Oh dear, yes, I've done it all, but now I'm begging for redemption and I wanna be like a virgin all over again."

This born-again virgin stuff is really puzzling. Is there any other part of human development in which adults have the urge to roll backward? Do grown-ups wish to crawl on the floor again so as not be corrupted by walking tall? Do we want to go through puberty again and endure our voices cracking and oil glands bursting, scrawling in our thirteen-year-old diaries the miseries we endure? I can certainly understand people wanting to LOOK like they never made it past dewy seventeen, but who wants to FEEL like a high school sophomore again?

Born-Again Virgins, whether public figures or anonymous party queens, are strange hybrids of the prudes and prigs who can't really Judge and Condemn others until they've wallowed in the dirt themselves. When they were first real virgins, the BAVs were probably a lot nicer and less smug about pointing fingers and assigning blame. But since they blacked out on dope, hired a hooker, cruised a tearoom, and stuck their fingers up their asses, NOW they're qualified to tell everyone else what not to do. This isn't virginity, it is certainly not innocence. It's bile-bearing righteousness, served straight up.

There are two things that are intolerable about bigots—the first, obvious one being their hypocrisy. If the first stone were cast at them, they'd be buried in a hot minute. They are epitomized by the preachers and politicians who get caught with their pants down, leaving thousands who supported them, financially and spiritually, to feel betrayed and humiliated. Jimmy Swaggart and Gary Hart were only the nationally televised examples; just walk into any neighborhood and find the local version in full view.

But there's another vulnerable aspect to these bigots: namely, they don't know how to integrate lust and love. Their eroticism is FUELED by hostility, anxiety, and ambivalence, all of which they try to sit on top of like a giant whoopee cushion. There's a hole in their hearts that, aside from being a personal liability, is even more of a threat because that hole is being filled with a political agenda instead of faith. It is so strange for these people, who are invariably religious, to be so faithless, so lacking in trust and confidence. Their priority is to HATE the deviants, punish them, put them away, put them down. If they loved the sexual minorities, it would mean they had to embrace what they don't understand, cherish them because they are alive, and cherish their sexuality as part of our collective essence.

When I decided to put the Morality Police on the psychiatric couch, I talked at length to my friend Jack Morin, a sex researcher and educator who has studied erotic fantasy and desire extensively. He believes that left-wing and right-wing puritans have this in common: they are horrified by lust. In their eyes, a grain of it is as bad as a bushel. Lust, they believe, makes people do bad things, and therefore lust must be tamed. Proponents of sexual desire are de facto spokespeople for the dark side. However, as Jack pointed out, when lust is suppressed, its negative qualities ALWAYS get worse. "It's that Jungian idea coming up again—that if we suppress something OUT of conscious life, it becomes a shadow . . . and in its unconscious form it becomes more extreme, distorted, and ugly. It is a vicious circle—the more you try to control the shadow, the worse it gets, so the more you try to control it."

So what do these Lust Suppressors do about their own politically incorrect fantasy lives—because believe me, they have them, they are not immune. Do they make an exemption for themselves ("I can handle it, I'm morally sound")? Do they blunt its impact ("It barely crosses my mind")? Do they "sin" and then feel remorse ("The devil made me do it and it feels so good to confess!")?

"Lust is antiauthority," Jack said (which immediately made me want to make a bumper sticker). "It doesn't conform to the rules. In our culture, with its particular religious background, we have the belief that if you think about something, you are virtually acting on it."

"Yes!—'lusting in your heart'—my favorite ex-president's quote!" I responded, "Like what I was taught in catechism: a sin that was never performed, only fantasized, was just as bad as a real sin. You had to confess it all to be absolved and do your penance."

Wishes and actions, in our culture, are judged by the same standards, even though in real life there's quite a stretch between the two. There's especially a prejudice against sexual thoughts. If I have a temper tantrum and say, "I'd like to kill that guy right now," people are likely to think I'm just gassing off in a bad traffic jam. But if I say, "I'd like to FUCK that guy right now," they're more likely to think that I mean business. People are a lot less sure that they can control their sexual impulses than their other desires; plus, they think that if you follow your sexual desires directly, you're even more likely to follow other aberrant, violent wishes. People treat sexual freedom like some kind of crazy advertising: "Sex ahead: no limits!" We think that the price of lust is inevitably the loss of love, the loss of seeing someone as a human being, but that's not true. Losing love and compassion is in fact the price of suppressing lust's natural, original feelings.

The openness of lust, of sexual attraction, is often the way we learn to love somebody, and that's no small feat. It is very difficult to love people, even though our communal evolution and ego lead us there in many ways. It is so much easier to be impatient, to discriminate, to draw as many lines in the sand as we can. For even the awareness of not loving someone, of one's loss, is compassionate compared to the demands of shame and blame.

The worst offenders among the Born-Again Virgins are the ones who are calculatingly insincere, the ones who no more believe in God than they believe in getting caught. They lie, and they believe their own lies. Their understanding of political leadership is that corruption leads to power, and there is no better aphrodisiac. They are so flagrantly out of touch with their bodies and souls: we don't so much wish that they would change, but that they would just spit out the truth of their own brazen self-interest. *Don't tell us about the Bible, tell us how you did it for the cash!* Such self-knowledge and its expression would be refreshing—the only thing left that we could admire them for. It would be a step in the right direction for them to admit they fuck and suck, like everyone else; what's holding them back is that they believe in preserving that pleasure for themselves and their favorites alone.

Next on the spectrum of the BAVs are the people who have turned abstinence and disavowal of the body into their own temple of eroticism. They may not be touching themselves or anybody else, but their fantasy lives are overflowing with forbidden riches. Here's the thing about the Just-Say-No fanatics: in their public and private tirades, they are OBSESSED with longing for what they cannot have, loathing the temptation. They are masochistic and sadistic in their search for martyrdom and punishment; and of course, more than anything, they are pinpoint sensitive to the taboos their religious beliefs and upbringings have put upon the sexual realm. They must have an EXTREMELY lush fantasy life; so when these people occasionally write explicit tracts that include sex, they end up sounding like expert pornographers (Jesse Helms on queers, Newt Gingrich's romance novels, Andrea Dworkin's confessions).

Not only are the Born-Again Virgins obsessed erotically with taboo and prohibition, power and ambivalence, they are also tremendous exhibitionists. They've studied Robert Mapplethorpe's photograph of a bullwhip up his ass a million times; they can't wait to be the first one in the committee to pass it around to everyone else. They quote dialogue from dirty movies, they fill their reports with blow-by-blow reenactments of obscene deeds. The lunatic *Attorney General's Report on Pornography of 1986,* a right-wing Bible of sorts, includes more than 300 pages of unexpurgated porno in its rigorous efforts to display the evil it seeks to abolish. As I mentioned when it was first published, I masturbated to the Meese Report until I passed out—Thank you, taxpayers!

Even as we speak, it's our taxes that fund government sting operations: setups where the FEDS print their OWN copies of ancient pornography, posing as pornographers, pedophiles, mischievous children, etcetera, etcetera. They circle each other, "I Spy" meets "I Spy," until somebody who's actually outside this ridiculous jerk-off circle falls into their trap. A bust! The more you learn about them, the easier it is to see that the porno police are the sleaziest group of voyeurs and exhibitionists you could ever stuff into a peep-show booth.

The next time a public figure holds up a picture of some shocking sexual spectacle, my response will be, "Now we know what turns *you* on, but frankly, nobody asked." They are as nonconsensual as the most self-absorbed raincoater exposing himself on the subway.

Of course they'll respond, "This isn't about ME! I'm just trying to protect the CHILDREN!" We must face down these transparent lies the moment they hit the airwaves. They are exploiting children so as to get their own rocks off in public.

To the casual observer, I suppose this assertion might seem extreme, since these public-interest flag wavers don't literally have their cocks in their hands. But don't underestimate the power of eroticism. Pushing the public's erotic hot buttons is much more sexually powerful than sticking body part A into body part B.

We are all acquainted with how sexual energy can be sublimated and hoarded in the interest of charging ourselves up for another activity. We know all about athletes who won't screw, artists who live by muse alone. Although we know that "losing sperm" literally is not how one loses strength or endurance, there is ample evidence of how sexual energy and vitality enlivens and supports our most passionate endeavors. For politicians and preachers who have made sexual taboo their ecstatic pilgrimage, fighting against sex is the foreplay, and raving to the press is their ejaculation. Their afterglow is enacting draconian, hateful laws to punish more victimless crimes—yes, they get their few moments of peace before the urge to get off again makes them reach out and find another scab to pick. The next time these people open their fat mouths and start waving their new compilation of obscenities, let's tell them to stuff it! They need to learn how to deal with their own struggles with lust in a manner that doesn't destroy other people.

There's one last group of God-loving and sex-wary conservatives, and they really get the least press of all. Most of them are not exhibitionists; in fact, the very notion of exposing oneself erotically is so upsetting to them that indiscretion does not often get the upper hand. They don't pretend to be virgins, they are not standing on any soapbox—not because they don't believe in the same ideals as other conservatives, but because such activism and exposure would *ruin,* rather than enhance, their sex lives.

These are the folks who, in their marriages, really like sex. Their intimacy means the world to them, and since they believe they fit in with what's considered normal (monogamy, basic intercourse, perhaps oral sex), they feel justified in their conservative view. When they interpret the Bible, or a local political opportunist approves of their "lifestyle," they feel blessed and sympathetic to all the prescriptions that say everyone should screw the same way they do.

But here's where these "normal" lovers become intolerant. Far from wanting to tell anybody what they're up to, or looking at dirty pictures of everyone else, they feel like they've got a magic potion that is strictly protected by secrecy, jealousy, possessiveness, and absolute privacy. They know intuitively that absolute fidelity (in the heart as well as the body) is difficult, that the future is uncertain. Their reaction to that dilemma is "Don't tell anyone, don't ask questions, don't change." When their perfect sex bubble is rocked by the inevitable evolution of any relationship, they cling to their old notions—even though questions, communication, and change are the ONLY hope they have of surviving the growth and aging of their relationship.

Experimentation and change, for these lovers, are frighteningly identified with the very idea of BLATANCY, of being out of the closet, free sexual spirits. Though they speak about modesty and humility, that's a pious cover for their own fragile sexual self-esteem. A gay parade, for example, makes them feel like they're coming apart at the seams. And it's not really the "gay" part, it's the PARADE.

This fear of erotic openness and its potential bridge to chaos lies in many liberal "solutions" to sexual controversies as well as the conservative ones. It is the essence of the "Don't Ask, Don't Tell" social policy in the military and elsewhere. This motto of discretion can sound polite—the opposite of the subway flasher—but in reality, what it has meant is "Big brother will ask whatever he pleases, and your choice is to lie or face the consequences." It reinforces conformity, this happy face with a big stick.

Vanilla Christians, enjoying their scripture-approved sex life, may imagine that they are free from sexual ambivalence, may think of themselves as the sun, with everyone else circling and admiring, trying to get some of that "normal" warmth. But this is only narcissism, elevated to cloning.

I know it's a tall order to cultivate a belief in erotic potential and differences, to let consensuality and dignity be our guide to what's right and wrong. Sexual freedom has so often been more easily interpreted as some sort of consumer sale-a-thon, "Get'cher red hot vibrator and filthy movie delivered Federal Express before 10 a.m. the next morning." Or it's treated like some druggy summer of love, as if one moment everyone would be shedding their clothes and having a good time, and then the next thing you know, everyone's doing bondage in Saran Wrap until they pass out.

Sorry, wrong nightmare—as delicious as they are, sex, food, sleep, and oxygen are not DRUGS, they're the conditions of our human need—not a luxury item. Sexual freedom is the antithesis of conformity, insofar as it ushers in experimentation. As threatened as everyone seems to be by excess, our natural discriminations really do kick in at some point; i.e., if you offer everyone chocolate ice cream for breakfast, lunch, and dinner, people are not in fact going to go for it.

Erotic liberation IS frightening because it insists that not everyone is meant to offer the same things, to be the same way in the world. It is the voice of change and creation in the species. It doesn't guarantee a damn thing, except that the desires to live and to fuck are entwined as an article of trust, a drive far more inspiring than a virgin rebirth.

I
Love
Being
a
Gender

♀ ♂ ♀ ♂ ♀ ♂ ♀ ♂

I Love Being a Gender

What's a nice butch dyke like me doing fantasizing about a drag queen with a dick?

—Trish Thomas, "Me and the Boys"

I've been mistaken for a man a few times in my life. When I was a girl, it was on account of a stupid haircut, of course. My mother said long hair was impractical, that I wouldn't take proper care of it, so snip snip, put a bowl on my head and presto, I looked like the world's tiniest, skinniest nun—or a small boy. A man at the hardware store called me "son" and I cried terribly. On another occasion, the problem wasn't my hair; it was my height. My dance teacher said that I couldn't be a fluffy baby chick in the dance recital with the other girls, because I was too tall. She gave me the clown costume and told me to perform with the boys. That was the worst: I wanted to be a fluffy baby chick more than anything, I wanted to be a pretty, curly-haired girl with soft feathers billowing down my arms and a tutu on my hips.

I have at least three tutus in my closet now, and I haven't performed since 1966, so there you have it. I didn't come out of the closet as a femme until my early twenties; it was my second "coming out," and in a way, the first traumatic one. When I first had sex with a woman, I stripped out of jeans and a T-shirt to make love with her, and that's what we both put on when we said good-bye. We made love like the two virgins we were, very curious, tender, wet, and sticky, but no penetration, no submission; it was kittenish, and that was sweet enough. I had no personal grief about being bisexual or identifying with dykes; I thought it was the most marvelous thing, I thought we had all been born on a silky lavender wave of feminist bliss. I thought everyone would come around sooner or later.

But as my love life developed, I started to have my own version of being a lady in the parlor and a whore in the boudoir. Except I wasn't as much parading around as a lady, with my flannels and cut-offs, as I was representing myself as a hippie, a feminist, a revolutionary with no time for Revlon bullshit and fashion magazine neuroses. It certainly was liberating to laugh instead of cringe at articles like one I remember, in a women's fashion magazine, which suggested that THIS year's breast size was "tangerine," and that "grapefruits" were on their way out.

I didn't have lovers, male or female, that gave a shit about that nonsense. But the ones that I had the most chemistry with, the ones I fell the hardest for, were the ones that picked me up and fucked me against the wall, or pretty much laid themselves open for me to do the same to them. I responded to resistance, to opposites. As I told one new lover, "Someone has to be the boy and someone has to be the girl, I don't care which, but we have to commit."

Not everyone feels the same, I'm ready to admit. For some people, it's that narcissistic same-to-same elation that makes their sex hot. But for me, that's an all-technique, no-passion affair.

In my first years as a lover, I felt quite twisted; it seemed like the same/same ideal fit my idea of an egalitarian paradise, and my erotic theater between butch and femme was strictly Neanderthal. I read lots of books and went to lots of meetings that argued for eroticism without drama—a sharing of affection between "equals," with the equality not only implying intellectual and economic parity but also a disassociation from erotic differences, the risk of wanting to fuck or get fucked.

My private life and attractions didn't seem to change one iota, except that I felt guilty about it. My leftwing lovers and I seemed to have some unspoken truce about this: the branch organizer could whip my ass when I was coming, and I could arouse the Teamster captain's lips and tell him to eat my pussy, and the Rape Crisis Hotline butch could fuck me without ever taking her clothes off, and when we worked together and appeared in public we were scrupulously professional, one comrade to another. It not only preserved our working relationship, but it was also the trust that let us be uninhibited when we were alone. I wouldn't change those boundaries today in any way except for one: to acknowledge what we were doing, to have a sense of humor and well-being about it, instead of acting like we were hiding our most reactionary tendencies.

I moved to San Francisco in 1979, and that was the year I met the drag queen who could kick me out of my rut. I had never seen a man dressed completely in faux leopard-skin evening wear before I moved to the Haight in 1980. That's how Chris showed up at my door the day of the Haight-Ashbury street fair—with his friend Tede, who was wearing a magenta ball gown that looked like something Scarlett O'Hara had fashioned from another set of plantation window-dressings. "You both are so beautiful!" I cried, and though they heard those words all day from the crowd, I think they could tell there was something else—that was shock—in my voice. I thought I was going to weep. Here they were, boys in clothes that I thought I'd never have a chance to wear in my entire life, and from the way they talked, this was just one inch into their closet.

"I want to wear a dress," I announced, like I was about to reveal a secret crypt. My friends obliged me. I spent the day flaunting my new femme identity, and that night I picked up a butch in a south of Market fag club who took me out on the street to cool me off. Yes, the asphalt was cold and wet on my ass, ripping the back of my debut dress, and as her hand went into my cunt I said "Fuck me," not to myself but out loud to her. Out loud, it was an aphrodisiac. My new lover's cheeks were rough and I realized she shaved. She was half a foot shorter than me and I lay in her arms, afterward, like a rag doll with goose bumps.

The first time I was mistaken for a man as an adult was in a literary way, I suppose, since my mistaken accuser had never seen me, only read my words. I had a sex advice column in *On Our Backs,* "the magazine for the adventurous lesbian," where I rattled on about fisting and butches and buttplugs and what to do when your lover melts your dildo in a fit of pique. My sex advice seemed deceitful and preposterous to some of our lesbian readers, and one day I got a letter that said they had it on good authority that "Susie Bright is a man." This, of course, is the ultimate insult of the baby-boomer lesbian, when she thinks another woman has gone too far. The younger dykes wouldn't say that now; if you said "Susie Bright is a man" to them, they might frown just a little, like they were trying to remember something, and then say, "Oh yeah? I thought she was a girl last time I saw her." Or maybe it would be even more snotty, like, "Sure, well, she's done everything else."

My serious women lovers have all been butches, and pretty old-fashioned ones at that. They want to be recognized on the street as bulldaggers—not men, but dykes. It annoys them to be called "sir," but they have no intention of changing out of men's clothes or growing their hair. They hate the way their breasts look in clothes, they don't especially like looking at their tits, but they like their breasts touched, respectfully, by their lover; they wouldn't dream of cutting them off.

I think lots of straight people who've been surprised by my girlfriends—or surprised that I was with them in my heels and cleav-age—have this burn of annoyance afterward, like, "What do these queers want? They want to wear a dress, then they don't; they look like a dick, but they want you to call them a woman. Well, they can't have it both ways!" But that's where they're wrong, and even more than that, envious—you cannot only have it both ways, you can have it ALL ways, which is many more than two and looks a lot like in-finity. Recognizing who people ARE, what they are signaling about themselves, takes a little more time and a LOT less prejudice than most people have been prepared to greet the world with.

It's hard to find the spaces where gender is in the moment—a presentation of self, right here, right now—and it's made places like San Francisco a tender refuge. At one point I was so fed up with try-ing to socialize in mainstream lesbian bars—which seemed to be filled with girls in pastel golfing shorts—that my partner and I started hanging out at the city's most prominent transgender club. In fact, we decided to spend Christmas evening there, because there was going to be a buffet and a special show. Now this place was run by a bow-legged ex-marine named Francine with a voice so gravelly she would make Tallulah Bankhead sound like a choirboy. She was protective to a fault with her "girls," most of whom worked as pros on the street, and you had to interpret everything she said with a little sugar.

"Listen all you bitches," Fran roared—and nobody ever said "bitch" with more mustard—climbing onto a small cocktail table. "We knocked ourselves out for you this year, and you better not fuck it up." There was a smattering of applause, and the stage music started up. I wondered where all these people's blood families were, whether their families could imagine this new family.

I was on my best behavior. I was wearing an electric-blue se-quined mermaid dress, and Honey Lee was wearing her silver-gray suit. By contrast with the lesbian bars we could have gone to, this did not make us stand out in the least. The only way we weren't a perfect match to everyone else in the room was that Honey Lee was white, and most of the trans' escorts were black men, a little older than my date. Everyone was trying to get close to the stage, to their favorite dancers or lip synchers, and a tall blond with a fox stole knocked her Seven and Seven against my arm. My plate of miniature meatballs fell splat on her platinum platforms, and I started apologizing first. Blondie looked at me and said, "Who are you kidding, baby?" and moved her furred fullback self past my gaping mouth. I was breathless from putting two and two together. If you subtracted the drink, the meatballs, and the loose fur that was left on my face, I believed, as I whispered to Honey, "She thinks I'm a man! She thinks I'm like her!"

And she wasn't the only one. I didn't get busted until I went to the bathroom. Jesus, I've never been in a worse one. It was not a drag queen's vanity, it was a poor junkie's porcelain with no plumbing. There were two inches of water on the floor, but hey, we were all wearing three-inch heels, I could manage that. There were no doors on the stalls, and there was no way I was going to put my ass down on the toilet seat—it was too scary looking. I was struggling mightily with my mermaid, trying to brace myself just right over the commode—I had to pee so bad—when in waltzes this brown diva, treading water right up to the mirror where she could fool with her lipstick, and, incidentally, see me right behind her. Maybe she didn't see me first, maybe she smelled me.

"FISH! Is that FISH! Oh my god, what's FISH doing in here!" She screamed loud enough to stop something, except that I was midstream.

"It's a fish taking a piss," I said, fastening my garter. "This is the little girl's room, you know."

"Little girls! Have mercy! You're six feet tall!"

I sloshed out in mid-scream. I was humiliated and exultant at the same time. I had hyperrealized my femininity onto diva scale, been recognized by she-male superstars, and then thrown right back into the chum barrel.

When I first moved to San Francisco and started my femme life, I joined a group called Mainstream Exiles, which was a multimedia, radical collection of artists who called themselves queer before that expression became terribly popular. We used to throw these little shows in various dirt-cheap locations, one step above a lemonade stand with a curtain. A weekend's worth of events would include Amber and Cherrie reading their signature conversations on butch/femme roles, giant paintings of threatening food dishes by my friend Kim Anno, singalongs against the Christian right wing led by Romanovsky and Phillips, acid and acerbic drag-queen poetry, and the Brown Bag Theater, which was a feminist recovered-alcoholics troupe. I learned to run lights doing a Brown Bag performance because the lighting director was moonlighting as a budding porn star, and since THAT was a paying gig, she was leaving the Bags to me. I crawled in the loft with her and she showed me how to turn and change the lights: "See, it's easy."

Later that night, at the postperformance party for all the artists, people couldn't stop talking about how Tigr was "sucking cock," and what the devil did her girlfriend Randi think of all that. Randi was one of the most intimidating butches about town at that moment; I could just hear her in my mind, yelling "FEE FI FO FUM, I smell the blood of a porno slut."

Jeannie was also at that party; that's where I first remember being attracted to her. She had had some good luck and a lot of respect in the queer artists' community at that point; she was published in a pioneering lesbian anthology. I know it sounds like a PC joke today, but it wasn't at the time, not one bit. Practically all the lesbian literature at the time was "How I Came Out at Smith," by Buffy Biddlekins, or else the material was so ancient or so consumed with political rhetoric as to be unreadable. It was truly revealing at that time, the beginning of the eighties, to see what dykes were up to who hadn't been invented by the class values of lesbian feminism.

That cast party was the last time I saw Jeannie for at least four years. I started *On Our Backs* with my friends, I designed my own porn movies, kicked in a few closet doors. My crowd was still unwelcome in the mainstream lesbian community, but not as "exiles" anymore—it was more like being into punk rock before FM radio caught on. There were plenty of other happy deviants to associate with; our world was actually thriving, and the generation gap was on our side.

One day I was taking a break from work at Cafe Flore in the Castro district, which is a great queer place in San Francisco to sit in the sun and stare or be stared at. I was probably there for two minutes when I got a big yell from someone in leathers who reached down to squeeze me.

"You're just the person I want to see!" It was Jeannie.

"Hey there, I haven't seen you in years," I said, really thinking, "You never gave me the time of day before."

"I'm getting a sex change," Jeannie said, "and I just came back from my first round of hormones!" She looked triumphant, and I fumbled to offer her the chair next to me. I couldn't have been more surprised if she had told me she just came back from the moon.

"It's so great, I'm so glad I'm finally doing this," she continued, on a roller coaster; and as she told it, it was all promotion, no details.

Jeannie's uninterruptable gusto gave me enough time to figure out that she had come to admire me so much because of my outrageous magazine. Since we were both appreciative of gender-fuck in all its lesbian guises, she expected a genuinely sympathetic enthusiasm from me. I was shocked, but trying hard not to show it, not let her see that I was just an old-fashioned femme whose pinnacle of masculinity remained a stone butch—a butch woman, not just any old guy with a dick.

Dick—that's what I wanted to know about. I said, "You know,

Nan at the office told me she seriously considered a sex change, but the cocks they give you are apparently so fourth-rate, she just didn't see what the point was."

Jeannie exploded in agreement. "It's a total fucking rip-off," she said, "They're selling pussies to guys for $10,000—any working girl can scrape that together in a week—but the cocks cost $100,000 for the whole procedure. No way, man, they don't want women to have cock, that's the deal."

"I didn't know about the price factor," I said. "That's a trip. I was talking about the quality, 'cause like Kate [another friend of ours] says that with her new pussy she can have orgasms in three different places: her clit spot and her g-spot and some other thing she called the t-spot, 'cause she thinks only MTF [male to female] transsexuals have it. But with these artificial dicks, apparently they're really small and it doesn't even work all the time—"

"Well, they told me five or six inches—"

"That is SUCH bullshit, haven't you seen Annie Sprinkle's movie about her girlfriend Les. S/he has this cock that's like a fucking tampax holder, I mean, she can't get off with it—"

"I haven't seen that movie," Jeannie said, and she looked a little crushed.

"Well, I could lend it to you, I mean, I'm sorry, I'm getting into all that and I don't even know what's going on with you. . . ." Here she was, telling me her big day, I'm the first one, and I'm arguing with her about her future dick size. I felt really petty; I also had a million more things to ask her, but not here at the Eavesdrop Echo Chamber.

We said we would get together later and talk, and I embraced her; my heart was pounding hard, like I was holding on to someone who was going away forever. I didn't want her to know I felt so fried by her announcement. She just wanted someone to be happy for her, so I was like a good mom: I love you no matter what! She told me to call her Joe.

The next week, I was at a housewarming party and ran into

Maria, one of Jeannie's ex-lovers from the old Mainstream Exile days. She was pouring a drink for her current wife.

"I have something to tell you that you have to sit down for," I said.

"Oh really," said Maria, one eyebrow floating up.

"Jeannie Herrera is getting a sex change and her name is Joe now."

Maria screamed like a car had just swerved at her. Her big green eyes bulged spontaneously with tears, and her lover put her arm around her. "Oh my God, oh her breasts, her breasts," she was moaning.

"I don't even know about that," I said. "She was wearing a motorcycle jacket, I couldn't see her body—I guess you must be right, you can't be a man and have tits."

"She had the most perfect breasts I've ever seen," Maria said, like we were standing over Jeannie's plot. My chest hurt inside talking like this, we were all hugging our arms against our chests.

The lesbian community had already been freaking out about male to female wanna-bes for years. Some dykes sponsored events that insisted that only "biological" women could attend, which seemed pretty mean to me, like they had decided there was some essence of womanhood that they had invented. I had MTF friends in the sex business who I had never known as men, and I related to them as women, period. They would talk sometimes about growing up trying to be a little boy, I would talk about trying to be a Catholic—it all seemed like something that could be overcome. I was sympathetic to someone feeling like a woman; I can easily understand clit envy.

But the desire to be a man—it was one of those things I knew was possible, but hard to place in my own body. The first time I ever strapped on a dildo, it wasn't because of some long-cradled fantasy—I never would have dreamed of it. No, it was only a dare, and as I adjusted the rubber flange against my pubic bone and approached the mirror in my bedroom, I felt like a genital unicorn, not a man. My image made me break down in belly laughs. I fared a little better trying to penetrate someone with my silicone cock. I enjoyed having my hands free, and the rhythm was the familiar rock and roll. I felt the tiny swell of a male ego expanding in my head as I stroked away— but when I miscalculated and the cock fell out, my embarrassment burst the bubble.

I kept making and breaking dates with Joe, calling her Jeannie on the phone by accident, which she did not tolerate. She seemed increasingly pleased with her hormone development, and told me she had prepared her whole family for it. "Christ, what did your granny say?" I asked her.

"She was really cool. You know, it was a lot harder telling her I was gay ten years ago. This just makes sense to her after that."

I could see her logic. My own gay aunt, who must be Jeannie's grandmother's age, has always discussed homosexuality and transsexuality as if it were the same thing, the third sex. My aunt thought it was preposterous that I could be gay! She said my eyes were "like a little doe's, so feminine. Who could ever imagine you another way?" For me to insist that I could be a doe-eyed femme and queer to boot was absurd to her.

Six months after we first met at the cafe, Joe and I finally had a date to meet at a gay lounge that seemed to be in the middle of transforming to a lesbian bar—a fitting locale. The barroom sits like a crown overlooking the heart of the Castro, a second-story Victorian with all the outer walls turned into windows and decks, the sun flooding in on any pretty afternoon. We arranged to meet at two in the afternoon, and I ended up running up the stairs, twenty minutes late. I looked around the room, squinting, but I didn't see Joe. There were only about five people there, plus the bartender, and I could only scrutinize them so much for clues. Shit, I honestly didn't know

what s/he looked like! Her dark hair—she never talked about changing that—her hair was something to look for, but everyone here was
fair-headed. I asked the bartender for a Dubonnet and told him I was
supposed to meet someone earlier—had anyone come looking for
me?

"Is it a man or a woman?" he said.

"That's a good question—I don't know—never mind."

I should have known to just stand still for a minute. A great
laugh came from behind me, and I felt Jeannie's hands on my shoulders. "There you are! I was just in the can," she said, pointing triumphantly to the men's room door.

"How did it go?"

"Fine. It's been fine for about a month now, even though I'm still
thinking about it in my head, you know, like in the subway station
john, are they going to bust me, is everyone looking at me—but you
know, no one's noticing except me."

I took my time to notice him, and s/he let me look her up and
down. S/he had changed—yes, a lot had changed; s/he was wearing
men's clothes, not unisex jeans and boots, and her complexion had
changed, her hair. S/he looked like a man, a soft, decidedly un-macho
man; she didn't look like a bulldagger anymore.

We took our drinks to a table and she barely stopped talking. "I
am so fucking horny, that's the thing you know with these hormones,
I feel like raping Bo Peep, it's unbelievable."

I realized as soon as she said Bo Peep that I must've looked an
awful lot like a lamb chop to her at that moment. She wasn't just
confessing to a comrade; she was turned on. That's when it hit me: I
wasn't attracted to her anymore. I was hot for a butch dyke with long
hair, full lips, smooth skin, and Levi's; a femmy guy with a beard and
a suit left me cold. My face felt hot with such a peculiar self-
knowledge. I was ducking and weaving through all her come-ons, because for me, the thrill was gone, but I had no intention of bringing
her down.

"Listen, I have to ask you one stupid question," I said, and she nodded like I could have anything I wanted.

"I know you want to connect with me because you know I'm one of the few dykes, or really anybody, in this town, who isn't going to sit here and condemn you or pitch a fit."

She opened her mouth as if to tell me about a hundred others who HAD pitched a fit, but I stopped her.

"And I know this sounds like some straight fool telling you if you'd ever met the right man, you wouldn't be gay—but I have to ask you: Before you did this, before you decided to make the change, did you ever have a femme girlfriend who loved your cock the way it was?"

She stared at me.

"What I mean is," I said, "did you have a femme lover, did you have someone in your life who respected your masculinity and treated you like a butch in bed, not like a GURL . . . 'cause what I want to know, if you had someone like that, why would you need to go to all the trouble, the surgery and the meds and all the rest?"

There, I'd spilled it. S/he could see exactly how unevolved I was now, how thoroughly retro I really am.

"Whoa," s/he said at first. "I never thought of that, never. I don't know if I have!"

My eyes must have crossed. How could s/he decide to be a man and not have considered this? Here I was, waiting for her to give me the hip rap on why it doesn't matter who you fuck, it's how you feel inside, and s/he's telling me that this is something heavy s/he's never thought about!

"Joe, c'mon, don't tell me the whole time I've known you, you were having little politically correct tongue lappings with clone-girls? Didn't anybody ever suck your dick, didn't you have anyone you really loved to fuck, who opened herself to you that way?"

"Well, yeah, there was one," Joe choked on her name at first. "Marina, we had that kind of relationship—I think—but it was so tied up with the drug thing we were both into, it's hard to tell."

"What happened to her, why did you break up?"

Joe looked really sad. "Just drugs. It's stupid. I don't know what happened to her."

I had to pull her out of that direction. "Well, I think you should take out a personal ad, you know, 'Adorable cock-sucking femme wanted for butch in a mid-life crisis.' "

S/he laughed—and then looked at me. Did I want to apply? No, I better move away from that proposition.

Joe and I said good-bye, and I said I'd like to talk to him again. I left the bar and walked home with the bracing feeling of being unsure about every single person I passed on the street—how did I KNOW who they were, how could I judge them or anticipate their point of view? I can't; I never could, and anything else is simply the comfort of fooling myself.

I thought about some of the first transsexuals I'd known, and how I'd only met them AFTER their change. Their post-identity was how I accepted them, but I didn't just think, "Oh now you're an XX or an XY"—I thought of them as bigendered, as having led some essential parts of both a man's and a woman's life.

The initial surgical breakthroughs that made "sex changes" possible decades ago created a couple of celebrities like Renee Richards and Christine Jorgensen. When the public learned about their wish to change themselves, the subjects always emphasized that their desire to be "the other" came from the deepest place—that their superficial appearance had nothing to do with how they felt inside.

But what I find, more and more, is that some people don't want to switch to their genital opposite—no, they want to liberate themselves from gender entirely. They are coming to this place not out of a childhood wish or identity, but from the cumulative process of living as a woman, a man, a dyke, a fag, a straight girl, a bi man. They have been all those places and their identity lies in the mosaic, not in any fixed spot. I feel like I've had my own version of that journey, without the physical props, simply because of the assumptions people have made about me from who I hang out with—or how tall I look in a tacky evening dress.

Since I met Joe and said good-bye to Jeannie, another handful of my acquaintances have started going to FTM support groups. The cover girl for one of my books, who used to be the most drop-dead gorgeous femme on the block, went on to become a James Dean look-alike, and then to passing as a man who no longer gives any dyke signals whatsoever.

I have been supportive to my bigendered friend, but privately squeamish all along, wanting to ask the "stupid" questions and then not always getting the answers I hope for. I finally decided to make an inventory of everything that was troubling me.

First, there is the aspect of body manipulation, especially the kind where you cut, slice, and stick on. Now I have a tattoo on my shoulder, pierced ears, and pierced labia, but the only ones people see when I go to the market are my ears. All those procedures hurt, to various degrees, but I can't say they hurt more than the orthodontics I was put through as a teenager (my ultimate comparison for pain). Ultimately, they have given me enormous satisfaction, and I have never regretted them for a minute.

Then I think of all the people I know who've gotten plastic surgery that is complementary to their present gender: breast implants, face rearrangements, liposuction, penile enlargements, you name it. A woman removing her breasts is not as risky as a woman getting a breast implant, but gender traditionalists tend to regard the first as a tragedy and the second as a "cosmetic" procedure. I am personally terrified of the medical risks of these operations, just as I am of sex-change surgery, but the thousands and thousands of people who get these procedures every year are never called DEVIANT, only vain or perhaps insecure. In certain plastic-surgery-prone areas like Los Angeles, body modification is simply considered a good career move that anyone with middle-class ambition might consider.

Then there's the hormones. Well, gee, who isn't taking hormones these days? You've got women thwarting the effects of menopause, you've got the ever popular steroid set, you've got women on birth control pills. Aside from hormones, there are the fascinating psychotropic drugs that let us change our moods and experiment with our personalities, and finally the popular recreational drugs—which, ironically, have the most predictable results of any of the above.

Health risks or not, we are clearly committed to "changing" our minds and our bodies as far as technology and imagination will provide us with the tools to do so. We are not in a position to throw stones at anyone who has gone farther in their desires in the operating room than we would at the makeup counter—or in an on-line chat room.

When I separated all my grossed-out feelings about surgery and drugs from the sex-change picture, I could see that all I was left with was my original prejudice—why would anyone want to be a man? My friends who have chosen to change to men, or to bigender, could answer that question handily, and I believe they do themselves justice. I am left alone with my embarrassing little female-superiority conceits, a genuine wonder about what will happen to MY body in the future, and three little tutus in my closet.

Marry Me

I am not married. I have never been to a wedding of any of my own relatives, which is more a comment on the estrangement of one group of brothers and sisters than it is on whether they are the marrying kind or not. Plenty of them have gotten hitched, but not me.

My mother has one photograph and one comment about her marriage. "I wore a navy suit," she says bitterly, and she does look very smart in her suit, which doesn't have one speck of lace or flounce to it. She and my father looked like they were going to a fashionable office lunch, not a church. So I caught on early that a wedding is about a dress, a magnificent dress, a dress that you can look back on, regardless of what happens to the marriage, and say with some measure of satisfaction: now THAT was a bridal uniform.

My experience of growing up in the sixties and seventies led me to believe that the best way to undo the injustices and ridiculous expectations of marriage was not to get married at all. "Why let the state be your pimp?" my friend Spain wisely said (before he got married at long last). "Why let a man be your keeper?" was the more common refrain of many of my feminist mentors. Romance seemed cruel in the marriage institution, promising a future as creamy and puffy as that bridal gown, but instead laying down the institutional framework for the most slavish sex roles. You go to work, Daddy, I'll go to work too, and then wash the dishes and the diapers.

Deviation from the ideals of marriage seemed to spell D-I-V-O-R-C-E and a real sense of betrayal. Yet the sexism of marriage conventions was so rotten, nobody seemed to be fitting their roles anymore—Daddy wants to wear a dress, Mommy dyes her hair blue and makes more money than Daddy, Daddy makes excellent home-made pasta and doesn't care if he ever mows the lawn again—these examples may sound silly, but people's real lives were even more idiosyncratic and unexpected.

When I meet couples who are married and still close partners after many years, it seems like a success in spite of their archaic marriage vows and youthful stereotypes of themselves. To be lasting friends, to be a devoted lover to your dearest friend, to accept someone with your whole heart through all the decades of change and fate—this was something that the dress, no matter how many ruffles it had, was never meant to cover. I would call their families a success in spite of the convention of marriage, not because of it.

So imagine my surprise when all my most radical friends started getting married in the past few years. They were all younger than me, baptized in the youth culture's irony purification baths, critical of every establishment and politically correct maneuver. And these couples, these lovers, sent me invitations telling me they were committing the rest of their lives to each other. Naturally, they were nearly all gay.

Two years ago I was invited to participate in a queer magazine roundtable discussion on gay marriage—to debate whether it was an assimilationist het-sniffing sellout, or an equal right to be fought for with the utmost reverence.

"Gay weddings are for squares," I dismissed. "They're Presbyterians who don't get the point. They want to be sexual deviants but not have anybody know; they think if they march down the aisle, everyone will think they're normal, nice, and only tangentially homosexual. Oh, it's so boring," I told the editor, "I can't even bring myself to repeat my scathing comments at a roundtable. Don't gays and lesbians have BETTER things to do?" I said I might change my mind if he changed the topic to "Gay Divorces: Too Many Too Soon."

But then I got another surprise. My straight friends, and bisexual couples consisting of boy and girl, started creating their own wedding rituals too, and THEY were imitating the gay marriages—they were not going down to city hall. "I don't feel right getting married legally as long as gay couples can't," was one comment of empathic solidarity; but when I attended these ceremonies, I saw that eliminating the state was only the tip of the iceberg. These rituals were beyond "hippie weddings." They were intensely fierce rants and tribal rites, romantic in the most rebellious and pagan fashion, polemics against the status quo and simultaneously very public vows of everlasting love. The love was not necessarily monogamous, either; but the vows would inevitably speak of loyalty and perseverance, devotion in the face of apocalypse and repression, not to mention "till death do us part."

My friend, journalist Evelyn McDonnell, for example, walked down the aisle wearing a white dress, an electric guitar slung over her shoulder—all the better to play "The Wedding March"—and a gorilla mask over her head. Evelyn and her partner Lee Foust published their "wedding manifesto" in Evelyn's own 'zine *Resistor:*

> We have no representatives of religion here today because Lee and I believe we are all representatives of religion, our love for each other a holy act beyond dogma or creed, the wholest and holiest act in our life-dramas. Nor have we invited an official of the state, for there is perhaps no figure more odiously opposed to love's beauty than the face of the bureaucrat.
>
> We also believe our coupling is not more blessed than any persons' who choose to shelter together under the protective arms of love's embrace. We reject laws and religions that do not sanctify relationships between man and woman as equivalent to our own. Committing oneself to sharing life with another person is a deed that should be honored, feted, celebrated, sung about, shouted from the rooftops, and greeted with the ringing of bells and pounding of drums whenever, wherever, and however it occurs.

I just couldn't get over the wedding photo of Evelyn with a hairy monkey mask. "Take that, first-generation feminists!" I thought to myself. Not getting married at all was perhaps a bland way of copping out, when I saw what it meant to others who subverted the institution to bring out its most spiritual meaning: loving someone, loving that person without reservation, and declaring that love to a community of believers.

It's time to call out the courageous. Do we finally have the nerve to say everyone has a queer life? You may not be gay, but you know someone who is, you love someone who is; if you can't name them, it's because they're sparing your precious little feelings, and you'd actually be feeling a lot better if you could accept them as your own—because they are.

Our families, our friendships are made up of quixotic erotic individuals, and denying their variety and substance is the childish hysteria of the antimarriage prudes. When I speak to a crowd, I always assume that my audience is made up of queers, and queens, and virgins, and people with daydreams I could never imagine. I have FAITH in their sexuality as a creative guiding spirit in them; I know that they've taken their damage and are an undetermined blend of innocence and wisdom. If they find someone to share that passion with, what is there to do except throw rice and bless them?

Who would have thought marriage was, after all, about love? Certainly not the folks who argue so defiantly that gays and lesbians should not be allowed to legally marry. Marriage is about children, they spit, marriage is about sexual exclusivity—well, if that's what marriage licenses are for, then more than half the heterosexual ones should be revoked.

Some people blame women's liberation for marriages going cracked, and of course I'd be happy to give them first prize. Women don't need marriage to survive economically; if anything, the question is more whether men can survive emotionally and socially—they're the ones who got trained only to bring home the bacon, and not how to care for themselves or take care of others. Women and men also don't need each other's bodies in bed to make babies; and when they do couple, they don't have to just cross their fingers and douche with Coca Cola to avoid an unwanted pregnancy. Children need family, love, and boundless possibilities, but they can get those blessings from any gender, any age, any union. When called upon to prove these claims, I call them self-evident.

The funniest part is that the very people who fight against alternative families politically are often THEMSELVES the product of untraditional and unpredictable turns of events. Professional homo-hater Phyllis Schlafley dearly loves her gay son. Bay Buchanan ran her big brother's "patriarchy-rules" presidential campaign even though she is a single mother. Everyone knows that Mr. All-American, Ronald Reagan, has more Hollywood divorces and scandals in his family than you can shake an astrology wheel at.

The new radical marriages seem to be demanding not false promises but sustained intimacy in a world that might fly apart at the seams any minute. Heavens, yes, these postmodern brides and grooms have got stars in their eyes, they are convinced that nothing material lasts, that politics is a lying machine, that the system divides and conquers as fast as it can chew—but as long as we've got LOVE, BABY, anything is possible.

The arguments against expanding the legal notion of who can get married to who compulsively misses the point—the point being love, and how you can't stop it. Destination LOVE—no limits—haven't these fanatics heard a song on the radio lately? Don't they know about Romeo and Juliet? What makes them think that their discrimination is going to stop anyone from finding the way to their own heart?

I suppose the hate faction can count its share of successes, but is it fun to read the statistics of men and women who killed themselves because they were ashamed of being homosexual? Is it inspiring to sit in a hospital waiting room and gloat that the lovers of sick and dying patients are unable to see their beloved because they are not "immediate family"? Is it satisfying to watch a coworker's life fall apart financially because her family can't share the same benefits that everyone else takes for granted?

Families are alive and kicking, despite the fact that so many of them don't get called families—they get called perverts, sluts, gangsters, a hundred different epithets that mean "You don't fit mighty, Whitey, nice and tidy." The kindly insult is to call a nontraditional family a "broken home." But there is nothing broken about a couple or family that supports, protects, and believes in each other. That's what faith is all about—sticking together in spite of everything that conspires to drag you apart.

The stop-queer-marriage bigots say that it would be a bad example to allow anybody to get married just because they love each other. They imply that it will lead to worse things (hooray for group marriage!) or squander millions of dollars on people who get married for the cash and presents and don't give a shit (whoops, don't tell them about all the heterosexual couples who already did just that).

The antimarriage people—and let's face it, they really are ANTI-marriage and ANTIfamily because they want to REDUCE, not increase, the numbers of legitimate families—these professional homo-haters are really bumming about the symbolism of gay marriage. They feel like one wonderful statue is crumbling—Ozzie and Harriet—while another hideous one is being erected: Jeff and Akbar buttfucking.

They are upset to think about gay SEX, which of course no one invited them to; but they identify gay marriage so much with eroticism, they find it impossible to shut their fantasies down. In the fundamentalist line of reasoning, homosexuals choose their lifestyle because they get so much good sex. What else could be the reason? Queers get to have all this sex and no automatic babies, they just go to parties and parades all the time! Yeah, well, we wish. They need help sorting out their fantasies from their fears, their erotic desires and taboos from getting to the church on time!

The old symbols, so unsexy and Calvinist, are not going to be resurrected in reality, no matter how much they scream and moan. If America is the first country to acknowledge gay marriage, it is a triumph of love and civilization, an end to marriage as gender-based exploitation.

I wanna put that big bee-you-tiful dress on just thinking about it.

The Flower Conspiracy

I LIKE IT WHEN baby-sitters confide in me. I confided in my childhood baby-sitters, I exalted them, I asked them questions I wouldn't dare ask my mother; and since she didn't get home from work until after my bedtime, there was lots of time to ask questions. I asked Janie Eckert to make a list of every dirty word she had ever heard of, and tell me what each one meant. I asked Carla Rosen to tell me exactly what acid was, and why it could kill you. When she ran away to Haight-Ashbury in 1968, she wrote me and gave me a revised version.

So now the shoe is on the other foot; now I am the mom, driving my baby-sitter Sherry Stanwich home, and she is nineteen years old, asking me a question.

"Have you ever been on a diet?" she asks. And even though she is not asking me to tell her what "fuck" means, or to describe my first sexual experience, I know in my heart that this is about sex.

"That is not a yes or no question," I tell her. "I was on a real diet once for two days, when I was fifteen and as tall as I am now, only I weighed 125 pounds." Sherry gasped appropriately, trying to imagine my skeletal figure.

"For the first time, my tummy became curvy and I thought I was FAT; I had a hysterical reaction to my late-blooming puberty. I read in a women's magazine about a diet where you drink Diet Coke and sip bowls of beef bouillon, and I decided I'd try it. It lasted for two days, and then I just got really hungry and ate something else."

Then I told her part two of my story. The part of Los Angeles where I lived when I was a teenager was a hotbed of feminism; there was an actual women's liberation center in my neighborhood filled with leaflets and books and Guatemalan fabric pillows to lean on during the meetings and C.R. groups that filled the room all day. One of the first times I ever wandered in, they were holding a Fat Liberation Meeting. I am so glad they didn't kick my skinny little butt out of it, because it changed my consciousness on the spot. This was in the early 1970s, when criticizing the diet industry was not the stuff of daytime talk shows. After all, it was from a women's fashion magazine that I first got the beef bouillon idea. It was REVOLUTIONARY to say that fat was cool, beautiful, or that one's health was not a matter for an insurance chart to determine. I left the fat lib meeting a sworn enemy of dieting, and the same skinny girl that I always was.

I'm sure that Sherry was sick of my long story but I had to tell her Phase Three of my relationship with dieting. At thirty-three, a year after my daughter's birth, I gained twenty pounds and none of my clothes fit me. Vanity and weeping overcame me. I hadn't felt so vile since I first noticed my tummy sticking out when I was fifteen. Now it stuck out all the way across the room, my breasts were like watermelons, my arms looked like other people's thighs. I privately admitted that I was exaggerating, but I couldn't stop whining. This yearning for slenderness was some kind of sick throwback to the horrors of puberty. Obviously, aging and hormones were going to change me in all sorts of ways, the least of which was going up a dress size. But I still gnawed on my dissatisfaction and nostalgia for the "old" me.

I decided the interesting thing about my fretting was that some days I could sulk all day about my looks, and other days it never even crossed my mind. I had to decide to treat my mercurial weight-watching tantrums as a psychological curiosity, instead of an indication of what I look like or how well my body was doing.

Sherry listened patiently to my lecture. She had already been prepped with animosity toward diets from her feminist mother, who is only a couple of years older than me. She explained that there were extenuating circumstances for her diet concern: she was part of a dorm committee putting on a Valentine's Day fashion show for Spring Break, the express purpose of which was to dress up crazy, sexy, to be total exhibitionists. Every model was trying to find his or her fox-o-tronic outfit before the fashion show debuted—in a week. Sherry wanted to wear this Marilyn Monroe dress she had stored from her sophomore year in high school. "Realistically though," she said, "I'd have to lose five to eight pounds to wear it. Is that even possible in a week?"

"Don't bother!" I said. "Why ruin a perfectly good week? Come over and check out my closet; I have a leather merry widow in your size that will make you feel sorry for Marilyn Monroe."

Her face perked up when I mentioned opening my vaults. Most moms don't have a closet full of fetish lingerie, and she was not about to pass this chance up. I was also not about to pass up giving a nineteen-year-old woman some erotic confidence—something that is in very short supply today for growing girls. I'm sure my old feminist mentors from the women's center would have counseled Sherry to reject the whole notion of the fashion show, and asked her what the hell she was trying to prove flaunting her tits and ass on a dormitory runway: the old "sensible shoes" lecture. My answer is one that not every woman is comfortable with: that Sherry was valiantly trying to get some sexual attention, a valentine's worth of attraction, and that is perfectly normal and even admirable. She wants her body to be appreciated, in a special situation that is safe and fun, and which signals the promise of her sexuality to the peers she wants to attract. She wants someone to notice her under all her sweaters and books, someone who will make love to her and dig her even more by the end of it. It's not a crime or a weakness to want sexual attention, as much as society tries to make young women feel that way. If we weren't always criticizing and pulling the rug out from under teenage women's sexuality, they wouldn't be so vulnerable in the first place. They need mentorship on every level, including erotic role models of confident, sexually powerful women. It is a femme fantasy to be adored, to make someone light up. Not every woman feels that way—it is a feminine quality, not a butch one. But it is also a feeling that has absolutely nothing to do with how much you weigh.

There are two things that nip a femme's obsession with her weight in the bud. One is that, with sexual experience—her control over her orgasm, her awareness of what turns her on, her sensitivity to her lovers—she learns that sex has nothing to do with the fat myth. This is a tremendous revelation. Women's, particularly young women's, hysteria about being overweight is directly related to their sexual naiveté, which is way behind men's development. Romance is so important to girls that they think sex IS romance, and that their figure control is the mainline to that peak experience. Real sex and real sex education will quickly show them just how far apart those elements can be. Wholehearted sexual expression is the antithesis of anorexia and bulimia.

Second, when women have control over something besides what goes in and out of their mouths, they develop other passions, another kind of determination. Some women realize that with children, or meaningful work, or their art, their priorities shift. It's easy to see: Heroic women don't get on the scales.

If I was to make a chart of how much sex I've had, and how good the sex was compared to my weight at different times in my life, I would have to conclude that the bigger I got, the better my sex life became. With this logic I should go out and pile on the pounds. But actually, I'm not going to stuff my face any more than I'm going to deny my appetite, because how much I weigh is not the measure of my sex life, or my erotic appeal, or anybody else's. It's a scam that sex and success equal skinniness. But what's even more scary, more unfathomable, is that without any of the diet products, without the dollar sign paving the path of exploitation, there is still that yearning to be ideal, to be a beauty, to be sexy in an instantly recognizable way that your competitors will covet and your sexual targets will desire.

Feminism's traditional critique of the beauty myth is neither really novel nor intrinsically feminist. The feminist scorn for the beauty contest is modern rhetoric attached to the values of modesty, humility, of caring for people because of their inner beauty—not for their appearance, which, after all, neither lasts nor grows. We don't need to read a feminist manifesto to recognize these virtues; all of us have loved someone or been attracted to someone who was not a physical beauty, but who we could not get off our minds. If we can love another person that way, why do we think we can't be the object of the same attraction?

Beauty, pure and simple gorgeousness, is conspiring against us. Sometimes I think it is a conspiracy of flowers and butterflies. My daughter walks out into a field of mustard and lupine, poppies and monarchs fluttering in the air, and she says, "It's so beautiful." It is, the color is dazzling, the newness of those soft petals, silky wings—it's all so temporary, you want to hold it all in your arms forever. But in fact, all we get to hold are our reminiscences.

There really are beautiful flowers and beautiful people, and in most cases they are usually very, very young, and untouched by disease; and when they appear in sunlight, it can blind you. Youth and beauty are so imitated and envied by the elders, it's hard to remember when we were that age and that fresh—because after all, didn't we hate it? Wasn't it a drag being ignorant and dependent, and under somebody else's thumb? There is this moment that everyone imagines, where you're still young enough to be a babe but old enough to do something about it, the emancipated teenager! But that moment is either so fleeting, or so uncertain, that it becomes more of a neurosis than an actual place in time. Grace only seems to come with age, and that's where we're different from flowers: they achieve gracefulness new in the bud. People only grow toward it. Grace is age's beauty.

The disgrace of the beauty myth for women—and this is where feminist rage erupts—is that beauty is traditionally considered the only thing a girl has to offer. It is what a woman has to give the world—quick, sell it while it's still blooming—and she has nothing else to offer once she fades. Intelligence, strength, stamina, artistry, logic—all the qualities that endure—have been expected from women in their service as mothers, homemakers, wives. But like the talent-show portion of a beauty contest, all those qualities play second-string to the bathing suit beauty, utterly lacking the status that those same talents convey to men.

Women's intellectual and economic status has come a long way, but that very progress makes it even more devastating when women find themselves asked to step up to the equivalent of a swimsuit competition—often when they least expect it. The professional requirements for models, actresses, porn stars, and others who display the charisma of their bodies on camera provide only an extreme example of the dilemmas faced by women in every occupation and situation.

It's humiliating and often chaotic when a woman who is demonstrating her abilities has her desirability suddenly put on the line. She cares about both—she's aware enough to know it's absurd to choose between them—and yet, there she is caught in the headlights of the double standard.

What is tyrannical about women's relationship to beauty is not the beauty part. It's the FEMALE part, that Ambitious-Straight-Girl-Trying-to-Get-Some-Control-in-Her-Life part. One sure way to see the target is to eliminate all the women who aren't part of the bulimia/anorexia/tit-job epidemic; women who know they're never going to be somebody's trophy wife. The anti-trophy women aren't on the prize ticket, and they know it because they aren't on the middle-class trajectory that would drive them there. The anti-trophy girls know they are the ones with the womanly hips (and all the other individual characteristics of real women's bodies), who service and love the men who may like to APPEAR with trophies in public, but don't find them satisfying in bed or as family intimates.

The anti-trophy wife knows that if she is married it will be for love, or for good sex, for good housekeeping, companionship, or breadwinning, but NOT because she will be paraded around on some man's arm.

Class is not the only factor. Dykes are another group who, while being as vain as any member of the human race, are completely out of the loop with regard to body fat obsessions. Lesbians will often have their own version of the "fat" discussion, with some trying to draw a line between obesity and health, while others flaunt it all in glorious magazines like *Fat Dyke*. But even the most conservative lipstick lesbian position on body image is at least 20 pounds more lenient than any straight women's magazine would dare admit. Again, it's not because lesbians aren't interested in beauty and desirability— it's because they don't drag the twenty-pound weight of trying to please a man around their shoulders.

Now are men the ones who are enforcing the "no-fatties" rule so ruthlessly? Of course, as individuals, some straight men often feel like they have no control over what women are up to with their bodies and fashions—they think it's idiotic, it's part of their despair over the value of feminine concerns. Other men are tyrants about their lover's appearance, especially if they believe that having the right trophy will lead to their success as a man.

Men who are sexually experienced know that thinness is a special erotic taste—not the norm—and that a lover's body fat has nothing to do with how hot s/he'll be in bed. However, those same so-phisticates will readily admit that when it comes to impressing other people, a lover with a Barbie-doll figure is very glamorous, just like Barbie's New Corvette or Barbie's Dream House. It makes Mr. Big look like he's got a fabulous possession, it makes his world look PHAT.

In other words, men tend to think of the beauty trip as either a burden on their wallet and patience or an opportunity to fatten their wallet and their ego—but it does not lead them to consider or reflect on their own body image.

The striking exception to this consciousness is the gay aesthetic, which is personified by the example of a man who appreciates beauty in himself and other men; a man who notices beauty, who seeks to attain it and build a whole environment around it. Of course, this view of beauty can range from genius to queen-size neurosis, but it's noteworthy because it is such a departure from masculine conventions.

Some men, regardless of whether they're straight or gay, carry the femme aspiration to beauty, even though the traditional man would rather hold beauty, caress her—not be her. There is a Hindu saying, "If we love sugar, that means we want to EAT sugar, not to BE sugar." The nontraditional man, eager to be cute and desirable, is typically labeled queer, effeminate—or a teenage rock idol. As insulting as that may seem to some, it is queer, triumphantly queer, for men to be beauty queens. They're actually doing the rest of us a favor, aside from looking pretty themselves. The more men care about their own beauty, the less heavy the trad-feminine cross is to bear. Since they haven't been raised to think that they HAD to know how to apply lipstick, when they approach the vanity table, they come only with wild aspirations, not a fear for their futures in men's eyes. They are daring to be adorable, not living up to the *Cosmopolitan* Code. Their training led them to believe that they had to ignore their appetite for beauty except as something to possess in another, never to cultivate in themselves. Cruel, cruel! Let a thousand penises bloom, let them feel like priceless *objets d'art*. Let's treat that beauty pedestal like the piece of old furniture that it truly is. It is not so high that anybody can't get easily up and down from divinity.

Spankful

I AM READING THE story where Frances won't go to bed, *Bedtime for Frances*. Little Frances Badger keeps getting up to tell her parents there's a monster in the room, an evil crack in the ceiling, a ghost at the window. Finally, after being woken up one too many times by Frances's bedtime phobias, her father growls in his sleep and says, "Do you know what will happen if you don't go to sleep right NOW?" "I will get a spanking?" squeaks Frances, who barely stands still for his affirmative answer before she rushes back to her room.

My daughter puts her fingers on the page and stops me from turning it. The picture on that page has Daddy in bed with a cross look on his face and one eye open.

"I wish they would show the part where Frances gets a spanking!" she says, with sadistic glee in her eyes.

"You're awful. I suppose you want to hear Frances cry like a big baby, too!" I say, just adding to her zeal.

I don't know why children are so comforted by the dramas of others' misfortune. Nothing calms my daughter down like hearing about how I got in trouble when I was a little girl, what foods I refused to eat, how I started screaming in the post office and just wouldn't stop.

When I was small and first attended Catholic school, I was so fond of one of the strictest nuns—because her great talent was in telling stories of martyrs and sinners that would curl your hair, they had such vivid detail and suffering. I had no problem discerning the moral of the horror stories, but I only felt the greatest pity and compassion even as I learned that the sinners had received their just fate.

Kids love stories and pictures about terrible crimes and punishments; they are fascinated by deep sensations and strong emotions, even though they have a terrible time learning to take the flak for their own mistakes. They will cry their hearts out not only over a real spanking but even over a mean look from someone they love. They will even endure unbelievable abuse from someone if they think of that person as their lifeline to love and acceptance.

I understood child abuse, and just the general agony of being a child, period, long before I understood anything about the potential eroticism of pain or the sexual desire to submit and suffer. When I'd hear about people who were "masochists" or "sex slaves," they sounded like very sad freak shows to me. I imagined that if those people were "loved," they would get better. I certainly thought I would get better and better—and let go all my secret humiliating fantasies, if I cultivated a healthy, normal sex life.

Years later, I learned that what constitutes a "healthy, normal sex life" isn't the content of your fantasies—which will cover every notch and kink of human experience and drama—but rather how you handle those feelings: Are you at ease with your fantasies and boundaries, or is your impulse to lie, deny them, suppress them? I learned about erotic fantasies partly because I became a student of sexual psychology. But I also cultivated some wonderful friends, who, simply by sharing their fantasies freely with me, made me realize that I wouldn't turn into an evil pumpkin or a sick puppy as a result of my erotic thoughts.

My friend Charmaine, for example, is a wonderful example of a woman who couldn't care less about conventional courtship and monogamy. She grew sick of the lesbian dating scene: things weren't moving quickly enough for her, or, as she put it, "I'm not trying to go into escrow, I just want to get laid." In her impatience, she had enough curiosity to start checking out the play-party scene in town. Typically these parties take place in some large studio or warehouse that's been outfitted with lube, rubber sheets, massage tables, condom trays, dentist chairs—you know, everything you need for a sex funhouse. In Charmaine's case, she was going to the female-only clubs, which meet a lot less frequently than the boys' nights, so the women involved tend to spend all month building up to it like a menstrual cycle.

She called me after one all-nighter to give me a blow-by-blow of the party proceedings. There was one woman on the rack, she said, and there were a few people doing ropes and tricky bondage things. She said one girl was getting an elaborate skin piercing that was woven together like a filigree with fine thread. There were all manner of spankings and whippings going on in each room. She watched a woman being mummified in Saran Wrap, which took forever and resulted in a five-foot chrysalis. Aside from all the trappings and wrappings, it sounded like Charmaine was in the center of an endorphin whirlpool—the bright eyes, the sweat, the heavy breathing as the torture rained down. There were only a few expert tops dishing out the various techniques, but everyone was looking to shine in the bottom's throne. The evening's unstated proposition was to see if you would give it up, how much strain could you take, what visions would you see.

I had to find out one thing she hadn't covered in her story. "Not to be crude, but was anyone just getting it on, you know, fucking, sucking?"

"Hell, no," Charmaine replied, "that was what was so weird. It was like being with a group of guys on the field, you know, competing for who could take the hardest hit."

"Yeah, the women have more endurance." I said, "I'll never forget a 'charity slave auction' I went to where this girl said she was offering 'fifteen minutes to make me scream' and no one could break her down. She raised something like a thousand dollars for the benefit."

Most people start out talking about S/M in a kind of cream-puff fashion, just to warm the newcomer up to its possibilities. In the past, I've been just the cream puff to do it: I'm the perfect example of someone who has a million kinky fantasies that I have no intention of ever performing. I love to imagine being a submissive, degraded, punished damsel in gang-bang distress, but in real life I can barely take the softest spanking. I'm an S/M tiger in my dreams, but a wuss between the sheets. I know how much the flavor of S/M, the threat of pain, can create sexual tension—how small, silky fetishes can create just as much psychological action as chain restraints. But I've always felt a bit guilty to simply defend the cream-puff division; it can too easily skirt the most confounding question about S/M, which is, why would anybody want to get hurt?

The simplest answer to that is the sensualist response, "because it feels good." But to those who have not recognized or experienced the diabolical relationship between pain and pleasure, this may not seem believable. Nonetheless, people are into pain—more than ever—because it feels good; they have not been brainwashed or blackmailed into such a state.

It's not about walking into a room and having somebody cold-cock you, any more than eating meat is about being served a bowl of raw hamburger. Pain is as slippery as sweat, and combines with your hard-on and your desire into a very powerful emotional and physical potion. Being threatened, and the pain of illusion, of terror, is erotic in many situations. In fact, fear and anger produce the same exact physiological response as sexual arousal. That's why the "fight and fuck" stories that perplex so many people are so common.

I always believed that S/M aficionados were perfectly legitimate, but I had only a primitive idea of what made someone get off that way. I thought, in my tender years, that if you slapped people across the face and they had an orgasm on the spot, that meant they were masochists, and if you got off delivering the blow, then you qualified for sadist's stripes. My first personal S/M experiments had this exact flavor, like some junior chemistry set blowing up in my face.

In the early eighties, I attended a big gay political convention, ostensibly to form a grassroots campaign against the "moral majority." Instead of focusing on how to beat the right wing at their own "family values" game, the group became bitterly divided over whether defending the rights of sexual minorities included people who were into S/M, bondage, cross-dressing, sex work, and assorted other sexual preferences that go beyond vanilla homosexuality.

Well, I'm one of these "United we stand, divided we fall" types, so I was heavily defending all the kinds of sexual love and life, even though I had never tried my hand at anything "extreme." I was disgusted when people assumed that because I was defending a political position, it must mean that I was doing these naughty things in private. At the time, it was fashionable among lesbians to insist that any kind of kinky behavior was strictly male, that women would never act out or defend this kind of sexuality. Their faction demanded civil rights for buttoned-down homosexuals and maligned everyone else. Oh, I hated them.

But when I got back from the conference, I felt a little queasy. Was there really something so bad about S/M, some darker force? If I only knew, would it cause me to give up my militant demands for sexual liberation? I asked my girlfriend at the time—well, demanded—that we do an S/M scene, and prove once and for all what was right and wrong.

I told her to tie my hands and legs to the bed and then use her imagination. The ties she used cut into my skin a little bit and my feet were cold. I was uncomfortable already, and it felt like being uncomfortable in a doctor's office, not in my lover's bedroom. She took off her belt and started tapping and then slapping my thighs with it. So far this was about as much fun as a poke in the nose. I gave her a dirty look, and she shrugged her shoulders, as if to say, "Well, what else am I supposed to do?" She lit up a cigarette and went to look out the window for a minute, which I gathered from my reading of S/M erotica was supposed to drive me wild with masochistic anticipation, but instead just irritated the hell out of me. "Angel, come back, try something else," I said, determined to give it the college try.

In a burst of inspiration, she walked over to the bed and flicked her ash on my belly. I screamed, which she took as encouragement. Bending over like she was about to torture an ant, she held her burning cigarette close to my forearm, enough to singe the hair and make a disgusting smell.

"God damn it, cut it out !" I said, and I swung my other arm so hard to block her that I broke my restraint and connected with her face. My face was red, I was furious, I felt like beating her to a pulp for hurting me like that. What the hell had I done to deserve it?

She looked so shocked and hurt, sprawled on the floor. I knew this was deranged, my demanding to be taught the finer points of masochism and then going apeshit. I apologized, she apologized, we licked each other like little kittens and curled up together to go to sleep. I decided I would figure out what to do about S/M tomorrow. It didn't seem like the heart of darkness to me; it was more like falling down the stairs. But maybe I was missing some key ingredient.

The next morning I woke at dawn, Angel asleep in my arms, her soft red hair across her face, her lips parted, all warm and silky. I had this incredible desire to DO something to her. I had this incredible desire to be mean. I was filled with mischief and trickery, guided by forces I can't explain to this day. I rolled her over onto her back, so her breasts lolled over to her sides, all plump and perfect and freckly. She wouldn't wake up for anything. I ran over to my dresser and dug around in my accessories drawer until I had a handful of silk scarves. I also found a razor blade, which I took into the bathroom and, just as in a prison movie I saw one time, I scraped the end of the razor back and forth against the porcelain of the toilet tank cover until it was entirely dull.

The scarf was easy to tie around her limbs and secure to my iron-post bed. I didn't make them tight, because I still was not ready for her to wake. She wouldn't realize she was restrained until she needed to move more than a few inches.

I slid in bed beside her and pulled back the covers down past her cunt, as red as the top of her head, and I squeezed her lips together, just a little, just so that I could feel the pillow of her clit inside. She made a little groan but didn't open her eyes. What a spoiled baby— she thought I was going to fuck her awake as I did every morning; well, surprise, surprise. I opened her labia further with my fingers, and she was soaking wet. The moment my fingers played at her center, she started to push up to me. Talk about a cream puff. I laid my razor's edge right at her bulging clit and pressed down.

"Oh!" she said, and her blue eyes flew open; she looked first at my face, then down her belly to see me holding the blade at her cunt. Of course it didn't bleed, thanks to my prop preparation, but it looked and felt like the real thing in every other respect. Her eyes teared up, and for one second I saw myself: What a cruel bastard, how could I do this to her?

"Oh, god, please fuck me," she whispered, the words leaking out of her mouth as thick as the cream coming out of her vagina. Yes, it was that simple, that pornographic; she pushed her hips up again, against me, against my hand and the blade. I knew at once she wanted to keep her eye on it, so I spread her even further, I braced her lips open on one side with the razor, and I entered her with my other hand, so quickly that my whole fist was in before I could think of it. I fucked her and swore at her, I told her she'd never get away with what she'd done to me the night before, I was going to cut her little clit off for being such a bitch, and the obscenities and threats poured out of me like I was speaking in tongues. The more she moaned and thrashed, the easier it was for me to speak. She was digging it so much that it made me feel like God on an S/M holiday. All I had to do was follow the flame.

She came faster than she wanted to, harder than she wanted to, her cunt shutting down on my hand so hard and tight I almost feared she'd broken my fingers. I had to let her relax before I could draw myself out, so I just embraced her as best I could with one arm, throwing the razor on the floor, kissing her a whole bunch. With her climax breaking my spell, I felt I had to tell her I loved her a million times, that I would never really hurt her, the toilet tank blah blah blah—but she seemed entirely at ease, like she'd known it all ahead of time. She was just waiting for me to make my debut.

Soaking Feminism

IT STARTED LIKE THIS: one fall I was running around the East Coast doing a book tour. I had two engagements in New York, one at the Lesbian Herstory Archives in Brooklyn and one at Alfred University, a small art school upstate.

The Archives are housed in a classic brownstone, every corner filled with dyke-related books, photographs, music, and even old clothes that lesbians used to wear—a collection of ephemera and a living library for lesbian life in the United States. On this occasion, the living room was packed with dykes of all types—black and brown and white and young and old—all ardent feminists. I had a new book and lots of stories to tell, and the only problem was time. I asked, "Should I read the story about sex and the single mom? Or my thoughtful treatise on the antipornography tracts of Catherine MacKinnon?" A terrible tension greeted my question, and then a couple of small voices said, "Catherine MacKinnon."

I laughed and warned them, "Now you're going to get it. You really would love nothing better than a down-and-dirty discussion about how to pick up a girl on a Saturday night, find her G-spot and drive her insane, but instead you're going to drive YOURSELVES insane by telling me you would rather discuss feminist theory." A few cunt-aching groans came out of the audience, answering my suspicions about their shyness. "That's okay," I said, "we'll figure out a way to do both."

The next day, I traveled to a rural upstate arts college. This time I faced a more homogeneous group, all young, all ardent, all white, not necessarily feminist. I posed the same teasing question to them: "Where do you want to begin," I asked, "with my dildo questionnaire, or with Catherine MacKinnon?" A tense silence came over the room again, but this time I was wrong about my estimation of its source. Someone finally spoke up: "Who's that? Catherine Mac-who?" Everyone else looked relieved that they didn't have to ask the ignorant question.

WHO'S SHE? Who's the high priestess of the feminist status quo? Who has exorcised women's sexuality out of women's liberation—as well as anyone who cares to protest her point of view? I didn't throw these accusing questions back at the wondering student, but I had to pinch myself before I went on; something had changed here, and it couldn't all be blamed on lower SAT scores. These students were just as interested and conflicted about sex, masculinity, femininity, and erotic expression as I was when I was their age, as anyone would be about the first years of their adult sexual consciousness. But their popular culture is different from the one that surrounded me in school; they were missing the baggage that I carried on my shoulders, my defensive feminist reflex, the alarm system that links sexism to sex.

These art students' first exposure to pornography wasn't a terrifying sideshow about "snuff films"; it was more likely a video their parents or baby-sitter had left out on the VCR. Perhaps their parents didn't RENT sex videos, maybe they MADE one with their camcorder—or, let's get real here for a minute—who's to say that one of their family members was not already a working member of the sex business?

A professor friend of mine, Constance Penley, who started teaching a genre film class on pornography at the University of California at Santa Barbara, told me that every time she offered her class, one or more students would visit her office and offer, "I have an uncle/cousin/sister who works at XXX company, and they would be happy to come to talk to the class about the behind-the-scenes porn biz." Constance went from thinking "What a coincidence!" to contemplating that in the L.A. vicinity, where thousands of people are employed by the adult entertainment industry, she should only expect her students to have family connections to the subject.

When undergrads today admit they don't know who the architect of the feminist antiporn movement is, it doesn't mean they don't know what feminism stands for—they just don't assume that feminism is automatically suspicious of erotica. They are very free indeed with their opinions about porn—the movies that they think are boring or laughable or filled with creepy guys and supernatural girls—but they dispense these opinions, good and bad, the same way they'd tell you about the music that's being played on FM radio. Some porn, they'll tell you, is radical, some of it sucks, and some of it is bogus—and some of it gets under your skin no matter what you think. That's an accurate assessment. They don't even call it pornography either—too long—they call it "porn," like a nickname you'd give a pet.

Porn as a nickname is so ubiquitous that now people use it to describe other kinds of imagery, like disasters (footage of earthquakes and floods) or spectacular food (*Gourmet* magazine). When I came back from the Big Island of Hawaii with a videotape of the lava flows I'd witnessed at Mt. Kilauea, I invited friends over to see my "fantastic lava porn," and everyone knew exactly what I was talking about. Porn is that lusty, obsessive, earthy stuff that we know will appeal to, or repulse, our basic senses.

I tried my best to give the art school students a little history lesson on the feminist dos and don'ts of sexual discourse. I showed them various porn images of women alone, together, and with men, to get their reactions. The female students had the natural responses of porn newcomers—comparing their bodies to the models, feeling overwhelmed by the actresses' over-the-top sexual appetites, feeling turned on or amazed to see someone doing what they themselves do in private—but they didn't judge their reactions at all by whether they deviated or conformed to a feminist sex doctrine. They think that applying feminism to a given situation means being as honest as they can be about their female experience, to listen to what other women have to say, to articulate a woman's concerns, regardless of what men—or other women—want or expect from them. Their intuitive consciousness-raising approach was absolutely refreshing. Why should I try to tell them, "Well, according to antiporn feminism, one of you is politically correct and the other is a tool of the patriarchy," when it's just a lot of gibberish?

Feminism is no longer a cult—that's the big news. Everyone has seen so many headlines saying that "Feminism is over" or that it's in its second and third WAVE, that no one except maybe the most extreme misogynist has had the balls to say, "What wave? We're soaking in it!" Women have changed every single notion about what's expected from them in the world, and men know it.

A lot of feminists are crying "What about the backlash?" And that's exactly it—you don't HAVE a backlash to ANYTHING until its goal has been successful. Movements that don't upset the apple cart never see one little dewdrop of backlash. Feminism, the school of thought that has matched the world's changing material conditions more than any other movement of the century, is part of every American woman's piece of the pie, however she chooses to chew on it.

All the political headlines that supplanted the cold war are about the sex wars. What is every political candidate's platform if not his definition of the status of women, the status of gender? Abortion isn't about babies, it's about keeping women's sexuality curbed. Gays in the military—isn't that really about how men don't have a place to be a Real Man anymore? The economy, you ask? Well, with 44 percent of American families headed and supported by women, you can't talk about jobs without talking about women's work. The service industry, the helping industries—by their very nature defined as traditionally feminine—are the only sectors where actual human labor seems to mean much anymore. The future poses the same question, one that has always targeted women, about children and their education: Do we infantilize them, idealize them? Or do we admit that if they are the ones tomorrow is riding on, then their critical faculties had better get a taste of power today?

Feminism as elitism is over. The camps of the straight superwomen who give their children hyphenated names versus the lesbian commune members demanding a gender-free vocabulary—they're individuals now, not icons, bless their pointy little heads. But women's liberation did get into their momma and their sister and their boyfriend; in fact, it got too big for the rules of a closely defined set.

The greatest thing that women's lib ambition ever started was consciousness-raising groups. What C.R. groups did was simple: tell the truth out loud about what was going down in women's real lives. And this telling truly set us free—the birdcage burst open when women started relating the details of their own pregnancies, miscarriages, abortions, and births—then all the ugly lies about a woman's duty, good girls, and sluts came to an end. When women talked about lusting after men, talked about wanting to fuck and get fucked, talked about wanting another woman, talked about their ambivalence about motherhood, and every other feminine-taboo topic, all the baloney about virgins and Madonna had to stop. Spelling out what women need from men, what they want, and what they get was a painful process. But it spelled the end of the romantic worldview of princesses being rewarded, punished, or ignored by white knights.

The second greatest thing the women's movement ever did was

to enhance women's ability to make money and take men's jobs. I'm deliberately saying this in the most threatening way possible. Given a choice between a white knight or his horse, the horse was clearly seen to offer the most freedom. It has been a game of historical circumstance combined with a lot of chutzpah, but women have taken their labor and their brains to every part of public life. Women desperately needed to show off their physical strength, their stamina, their aggression, their femme balls, and there's no greater inspiration for this than Gloria Steinem, Rosie the Riveter, grunge girl guitarists, the gorgeous ladies of wrestling, and the women who drive eighteen-wheelers.

Finally, the most physically challenging and intimate accomplishment of feminism was that it was the modern launchpad for lesbianism. I don't know how long it would have taken me to get around to sleeping with women if I hadn't read the feminist primer, *Our Bodies, Ourselves* as early as I did. Not that anything in that book was the least bit sexy. Status-quo feminism did everything it possibly could to make lesbianism seem like the most sexless intellectual exercise imaginable. But all those pious little articles about the superior lives of lesbians made you wonder what you were missing. If you had the curiosity and nerve to try it, which I did, the actual experience of lesbianism was so powerful that it really did bring new meaning to the word "sisterhood." To acknowledge your sexual power with a woman, to touch her deeply and feel her touch back, meant that we could no longer look at each other as competitors for a man, or as a daughter obliged to her mother. We experienced, in that peculiar zeitgeist between the sheets, an absolute equality, a world without men.

By "advocating lesbianism," I'm not talking about some special kind of "equal" sex where two women in identical tunics lick each other politely in timed intervals. Nor am I speaking of some silly fantasy that lesbians match each other like sweaters, or any other nar-

131

cissistic invention. I am saying that a woman who is AFFECTED by lesbians cannot regard her body or her purpose in life in the same way anymore. This experience is so pervasive and emblematic that there are now women by the scores who have not literally "done the deed" with any woman, but who are "queer straights," as culture critic Ann Powers puts it: feeling their oats lesbian-style, keeping boyfriends at home but going out with the girls for the lesbian big dick/big dyke energy. Why shouldn't they? It's infectious.

So here we have these accomplishments: consciousness raising and taboo breaking, invading the masculine sphere, and finally the age of lesbian chic—all of which were inspired by, but then transcended, the available feminist leadership. I've talked to many feminists my own age and older who lament how young women today don't realize what we went through, that they take so much for granted. But isn't that the point? Isn't that the best gift? Isn't it the greatest that our daughters are the shocking pink power rangers of the future? Look at all the time WE wasted arguing about whether you should wear lipstick or not, while THEY have already embraced every color of possibility.

It's a gal's world, but being "girly" and feminine has never seemed so nostalgic, so romantic, so kitsch. Femininity is fetishistic; it's so elaborate that we look to drag queens for expertise. High heels are no longer de rigueur from nine to five, they're a sex toy, very much in their proper place. I don't feel alarmed by gothic displays of feminine underpinnings. Now that the fashion world has come out of the closet, glamor and costume are offered to boys and girls alike, instead of the one-gender-straitjacket-fits-all.

I suppose I should be kinder to the cult of fundamentalist feminism, since I have been such an earnest member. I cried over things like shaving my legs and enjoying smut, and my inability to build my own organic composting toilet (still working on that one); I was one of the femmes who hated the constraints of femininity, and I didn't know how to get out of them except by hacking them off, each and every one. I hated being tyrannized by the beauty industry, I was nauseated by media depiction of bimbos and martyrs, and I wanted to save the earth, damn it! I feel the same way today; I just have a different way of expressing it. I share my lipstick with my boyfriends, I make my own porn with my pals (Pal Porn!), and I do my best to create something beautiful out of my garbage. I'm not typical of feminism, but I am a product of it. When I was in the "cult," I thought I had to follow the rules in order to belong; I thought small deviations could get me thrown out. I thought we were fighting a losing but heroic battle. That was so un-Amazon of me.

Sex Toys

♀ ♂ ♀ ♂ ♀ ♂ ♀ ♂

The Vibrator Clerk Chronicles

WHEN THAT BOOK *All I Really Need to Know I Learned in Kinder-garten* came out, I remember pausing to think whether that were true for me as well, and then shaking my head. No, everything I need to know I learned in a vibrator store.

I spent my most satisfying job years working in a feminist vibrator emporium in San Francisco, Good Vibrations, which in the early eighties was a very small shop, more of a missionary outpost than a profit-making center. I liked it because it was very slow; I could read all the sex books on the shelves waiting for one customer to come in, and then, since we were alone, s/he would usually take a chance and tell me what was on her/his mind. It was not the sort of place where people just drove up and asked for a Hitachi Magic Wand and plunked the cash on the table. People came seeking information, therapy, a clue. It was very rewarding to help them, if I could, and afterward it would gall me terrifically how much people were suffering for the lack of the most basic sex education, and how women in particular lacked confidence about fundamental sexual matters. I wanted to put up billboards; I wanted an emergency broadcast system to interrupt network television and tell everybody, "Listen, pull down your pants and follow the bouncing ball."

The biggest irony of the sexual confessions I heard was that truth-seekers came to the store barely able to utter their concern since it was so unique and knotty, but their questions were very similar. It was like the same five problems coming in all day, every day. If I hadn't been sworn to discretion, I would have handed out phone numbers: here, this is a list of the forty-two people from last month who have the exact same shameful secret as you. "This isn't a personal problem, this is a social problem!"—is all I kept thinking, and like so many other things about sex, the question that people walked in with was often just the tip of the iceberg.

The most common problem for women is orgasm, and their facility in bringing it about. About a quarter of the women I spoke to had never come, or weren't sure they had. But at least half were hamstrung by feeling that their orgasm depended on a very vulnerable thing, or situation, or lover, without which they were incapable of coming. Without their vibrator, or their ex-husband, or the smell of gardenias at noon, they couldn't get off. Finally, the smallest minority were the women who said they could come at the drop of a hat; if anything, they wished they could restrain themselves. Yeah, I envied them, too.

One of my most quoted lines is, "I never met a man who told me he didn't know how to come, or didn't know where his penis was." That pretty much sums up the dilemma of women's sexual responsiveness. Lots of women have never even said the word "clitoris," or touched their clit, and don't really have a good idea about their genitals at all. Their predicament is caused somewhat by our physical aspect—that our clitoris is usually more hidden than a man's dick—but the reason more women haven't gotten out a mirror, parted their lips, and taken a good look doesn't have to do with physical ability, but rather tremendous inhibition. Nice girls don't look at their cunts, dumb nice girls don't know what's going on below their waist. When I took childbirth preparation classes, and our teacher showed a few graphic slides of a woman's vulva and vagina to illustrate some point about childbearing, I could tell by the looks on some of my classmates' faces that they had no bloody idea that was what it all looks like.

Giving someone a map, a helpful book with illustrations, a video that gives facts as well as fantasies; that's all a teacher has to do sometimes—then wait for the gushing thank-you letter. But it's trickier by far to deal with the second group of women—and this is a group most women have been a part of at one time or another—who only have orgasms under very selective conditions: only with their ex-boyfriend, only on an extended vacation in Hawaii, only by rubbing on the Maytag in full spin cycle. These women may have perfect knowledge of their anatomy, but it's never more clear that sexual release is about your mind more than your cock or clit. In an erotically charged situation, you might have your panties knotted up in a ball or your arm falling asleep, but still come like gangbusters. If, on the other hand, your mind does not feel desire, you can have every hole filled, every vacation and vibration in place, and still be completely unmoved.

Without fantasy, your cock or your clit may as well be as erotic as your elbow. But fantasies are constantly trivialized, and demonized, in the sexual learning curve. The stereotypes are the worst: most people believe that fantasies come from one of two gender-related formulas. If you are a man, it's about the *Playboy* centerfold showing up at your door asking for a cup of sugar. She's buxom and she wants you. For the protofeminine variety, we have a similar pink-bubble scenario where a tan hunk of perfect proportions appears on the scene and takes us for a walk down a sunset-drenched beach, seduces us on white sheets, a fire crackling warmly nearby, a bearskin rug between our toes. As cute as that may be, it's not at all how most sexual fantasies work for people.

My friend Jack Morin wrote a book, *The Erotic Mind,* which is my current bible on the nature of erotic fantasy and how crucial it is to understand who and what turns us on. Jack outlines "four corner-stones" of eroticism: "longing and anticipation, violating prohibi-tions, searching for power, and overcoming ambivalence." These feelings come in every sort of dose and formula depending on the in-dividual. Bearskin rugs don't really have much to do with it at all—it's the context and feelings that are so powerful, the props are secondary. That's why those self-help books about "How to Please Your Wo/Man" are so lame: they're list-makers and cookie recipes, not the story of one person's contradiction-filled erotic thumbprint.

Let's talk about a real-life fantasy that touches on the corner-stones Jack describes. Let's say I find myself disgusted and exasper-ated by a certain coworker, who makes passes at me even though he knows I hate his guts. I realize I am slightly turned on, but the whole prospect of really getting it on with him makes me loathe myself (am-bivalence in spades!). Now let's say I never know what day of the week, if any, he's going to show up. I find myself staring at my closet in the morning, wondering what to wear in case he's there, wishing he was in a certain situation at a certain time to my liking, and know-ing I can't really do a damn thing about it! (So much longing and an-ticipation.) To my complete surprise, he shows up at a wedding I've been invited to. We play cat and mouse (power, power) all afternoon, and minutes into the ceremony, we sneak into one of the confessional booths in the chapel and fuck our brains out, his fist in my mouth to keep me from crying out, my fingers in his asshole pulling him to-ward me (violating every prohibition in the book, not to mention try-ing to bend the other to your will). After our blowout, we sit in that hot, claustrophobic cubicle in silence until the wedding parade exits and allows us a chance to sneak out. In those moments I am still siz-zling from the fear of being found out, my outrage that he made me come so hard, my smugness that I made him lose control, my embar-rassment that, after all this, I still don't like the bastard. This is the kind of contradiction-filled erotic experience that promises to linger in my sexual memory bank forever.

When you think of erotic moments that stand out in your past, do you think of the times you placidly lay down and assumed the position with someone who you had a perfectly sensuous reaction to, but never felt longing for, or ambivalence about? Someone who had no surrounding power or taboo? Of course not; such an experience sounds like processed food, not sex. Most of the time sex is not wildly explosive, or adrenaline producing, nor should it be: none of us could keep up, and it wouldn't satisfy our needs for intimacy, stability, or companionship. But even the HINT of these powerful emotions lubricates the erotic experience. When I am aroused, it is not because someone just methodically cranked my clit for an hour or put love potion on my nipples; it's because of my complicated feelings and past with that lover added to my fantasy life, which may have nothing whatsoever to do with the body in bed next to me.

Fantasy AND the right touch are the key to reaching the plateau before orgasm, that delicious place where you know damn well you're going to come, and it's just a matter of falling over or teasing yourself as long as you can stand it. "Plateau" is a funny sex-ed word: it's very descriptive of how high you feel, but it's more solid than that; it's a place you reach, and once you get there, it almost doesn't matter what happens, it's hard to ruin your incoming climax. The reason vibrators are so popular with women is because the intensity of that vibration on your labia and clit gets you zooming up to that plateau. Vibrators do for many women what a few long strokes do for a man. When I first discovered vibrators, I had vibrator races: I would see if I could come in under a minute, and then laugh like a maniac when I succeeded. I was giddy, and who wouldn't be, after all the years I'd spent taking half an hour to come, with my arm and fingers so worn out I could barely lift my wrist?

After the first flush of technological wizardry, I started to slow down—What was the rush, after all, when I wasn't desperate? It was then I realized that if my fantasies weren't buzzing, then nothing plugged in really made a difference. I also found myself in sexual situations where technically it was all wrong—I disapproved of my partner in some way, or it was an unattractive setting, or there was some insane dog barking next door—and yet, when my mind was engaged, when my fantasies were fleshed out, I could come like a runaway train. I realized that, as interesting as the anatomical information was, the only way people can really access their desire is to be in touch with what turns them on, and to be able to reach those thoughts whenever they are sexually ready.

So many people are ashamed of their sexual fantasies—or bewildered or nonplussed by them—that they only reach them by surprise, a sneak attack. I've had more than one lover tell me, "I want you to turn me on, but I want you not to let me know you're turning me on. You can't come at it through the front door; it has to sneak up on me." As a lover, I found that completely infuriating, not because I can't empathize, but because other people's back doors aren't necessarily the same as mine, and I can't deliberately orchestrate the keys to their unconscious without a lot more clues.

Men and women are both repressed about their fantasies, although men seem more often to say, "So what? I don't have fantasies, but it doesn't stop me from getting off." I know men have fantasies, but since favorite fantasies only take a second to recall, a lot of people don't notice them—they're on automatic pilot. Men can get aroused faster than most women, and their fantasy foreplay is shorter, although it makes just as much of an impact on how they come, and whether it's a peak sexual moment for them.

Men do not complain about not coming, but they do ask a lot about coming when they don't want to—and not being hard when they want to be. I've phrased these two complaints carefully, because in popular discussion, most people refer to them as premature ejaculation and impotence. Those terms are a big fat NO-NO among the sex-researcher set, because they are more like pejoratives, like branding some guy an idiot and a jerk, than helpful physical descriptions.

Virtually every man sometimes experiences erection when he wishes he wouldn't, just as he will not always get an instant hard-on when he feels desire. Having an erection, despite the general consensus, is not the absolute indicator of whether you are turned on or not. But because it is the phallocentric bellwether, because it's how many men judge whether they're happening or not, they can get a big surprise when—due to illness, or age, or depression, or psychological disposition—their erection doesn't lead the way of their arousal. Some men I know are truthful enough to say, "I know it feels just as hot to me when I have a partial erection, but when I look down and don't see it hard as a rock, it's a complete letdown."

That letdown feeling also occurs when a man comes when he doesn't want to, which typically means coming *before* he thinks he should or could or would. It's such an oppressive concern, but it's really about a big curtain call and not satisfaction. I know that I love to come before my partner, to be the "premature ejaculator." How can you be premature when it feels so good to let loose? I certainly don't presume that "SEX IS NOW OVER" just because I've come; that is such a straight hang-up. If a man wants to please his partner and also reach a climax himself at some other point, who cares when it is? Lovemaking is not, no matter what we've heard, about running around the bases. It's only if a man thinks his hard cock is the be-all and end-all to getting off that things start getting irritating. Maybe all young men should be given a dildo set at puberty, all different sizes, with a little card that just says, "Relax."

But then there's that more advanced situation where a man wants to stay on the plateau and bliss out, yet his impatient cock seems to betray him into coming before he wants to. There's a whole retinue of strategies you can use to change this situation, revolving around techniques of teasing, breathing, and stifling; and not only can you read about it in books, but you can watch it step by step on video. Masturbation is the ultimate practice-makes-perfect arena, just as it is for women who are having a hard time getting aroused. It is remarkable to see how you relax when you are alone, without judgment or expectations.

These first concerns I've mentioned—women wanting to achieve orgasm, men not wanting to come "too soon," and men wanting always to have a hard-on of steel at the ready—are the white-knucklers that divide the sexes. The next on the list, however, is universal. Whenever someone would walk into the store, and was just not able to say what it was, their face as tight as a . . . sphincter, well, it was best to just give them a good shove into the buttplug cupboards. More frequently, I would just say it: "Anal sex, anal sex, anal sex," until they gave it up.

It's ironic: even though butt-fucking is popularly associated with gay men in today's sexual culture, it is in fact heterosexuals who have gone wild about their asses. Ask anyone who works in a sex toy shop what single item has surged forward in sales in the past fifteen years: buttplugs. And dildo harnesses for women who are clearly involved with men. Anal titillation is also just as much about not quite doing it as it is about complete penetration. I had a brief affair a few years ago with a man much younger than me who bolted upright over my body when I first reached around to cup his cheeks. "You aren't going to do anything there," he said, like a pulp-novel virgin. "Well, I didn't have any agenda, but now you've got me interested," I said. He begged me to promise I wouldn't slip anything in, not even a pinky. His cock was hard as a rock as he entered me. I couldn't resist—I had to see—so I said, "What if I just put my hand OVER it, what if my fingers are right NEXT to it?" He was delirious with the almost-but-not-quite possibilities.

Here are the reasons that boys and girls are so crazy about anal sex: Number one, it feels really good, because it stimulates the prostate gland on men and the internal clitoral body on women. Both these kinds of stimulation can propel one to orgasm. Second, the deviance of anal sex, its taboo properties, make it explosive fantasy material in people's minds—it's just too delicious. Will it make you a bad girl, or a fag? Will it hurt, or will you get hooked? All these are fears that can be antierotic to the point of phobia, but it's that same fear/anxiety sensation that on a more moderate level can create peaks of arousal.

Anal sex brings out a lot of cornered positions. So many people want to be on only one end of the equation, to fuck or be fucked, and they feel they deserve that one position, period. I can certainly understand a preference one way or the other, but there's a stuck-up aspect to the man who can't imagine himself ever being the one who yields. It's not a stretch for me to speculate that men who have been fucked, who sometime in their erotic careers have opened up and been sexual receptors, are better fucks for the experience, and better tops than men who stand on macho reputation alone. That said, consider how many American men have been fucked, and how many women have taken the driver's seat, and there you are: the prisoners of gender are ruining everyone's potential again.

In the sixties, a favorite chant was "Everybody must get stoned," and it was a call to consciousness, not to a twelve-step orgasm. In the same vein, today everybody must get fucked, mutually, respectfully, from both sides.

Among the converted, this is not news, but I know that the many uninitiated—or people who've had a non-consensual experience—are beleaguered by this one. "Getting fucked" is our culture's routine terminology for being taken advantage of, screwed over, blown away. It is anticompetitive to get fucked. It is unfeminine to fuck at all. It is antivirile to open up. It is the complete ruin of the work ethic to be "fucking" your life away.

You know, I wish it were that simple, because a lot of omnipotent jerks have discovered the pleasure of anal sex, but they just go right back to the office in the morning and fire another round of missiles. They've carried out the practice, but not the spirit of the thing—

145

I don't think they've entirely missed the spirituality, they're just not honest with themselves. I've only met this type a few times, the ruling class in bed, and they always say, "God, this is so wonderful, so open and honest and uninhibited," but since they're SLUMMING, they get to have a big remorse bone to chew on afterward. The two-faced sexual libertine is just as annoying as the full-time punishing puritan.

It was always fun for me to hand people a bottle of lube and a book, and tell them how to enjoy the kind of sex they fantasized about, so that they wouldn't hurt themselves and would still have a gay old time. But what I couldn't address entirely is how they felt about the stigma of their sexual desires, the way sexual repression had affected their lives. Clearly the people who came to visit me at the vibrator store were in the mood to explore. But sometimes I'd meet couples in which one partner was there because s/he thought s/he would be abandoned if s/he didn't go on this field trip. That's when I felt like the couple should have been in the relationship shop instead of the vibrator boutique.

The only way you have a chance of talking your lovers into doing something experimental, when they're dead set against it, is to be the guinea pig yourself. Put the tit clamps on your nipples, the dildo in your hungry mouth, and let them watch. Tell them a story that arouses you. Let them see you get turned on. That is a gift. Your lovers may not see themselves doing the same thing, but seeing their lover so vulnerable, so true, makes a body awfully humble.

Aroused

I WAS INTRODUCED TO the IDEA of pornography in three different ways. For starters, I knew it was a men's club thing, boys only, no girls allowed unless you show your titties. I imagined it was a bunch of Type A bullies, chauvinist to the bone, who couldn't look at a girl without reducing her to a bra size. "Porn exploits women"—isn't that the first thing a young lady learns about the cold cruel world? It's a synonym for Men Use Women in the most calculating way.

Second, I knew pornography was a business with a capital B. Millions upon millions of dollars were said to be made at it; it was an industry with a lingam instead of a smokestack, blowing clouds of jizz and peep-show quarters.

My anticipation of what porn actually LOOKED like—as opposed to the money it made, the way it operated, or what it did to its talent—was that it started at cheesy, moved on to gross, and ended at its logical resting place: the snuff film.

My real-world introduction to porn started with these thoughts in my head, and the whole mess was so intimidating to me that I would never have taken a peek into it myself—if my new girlfriend, Honey, hadn't gotten a job working as a cashier in a large theater downtown, a porn theater that featured live strippers and classic X-rated movies.

147

Honey got the job because of Charles De Santos, a pornographic filmmaker she met at a party. They were both camera nuts and he spontaneously gave her his old light meter, which she thought was marvelous. Then he gave her a job at the Market Street Cinema, which he was managing at the time. When Honey came home from work, she told me that the whole place smelled really bad, and that she could chain-smoke her entire shift. She said there were some girls who were beautiful working there, some of them with mouths as smart as their stage whips, and some so sad you just wanted to cry. The next week she told me she went to change the lightbulb in the ladies' john, and when she unscrewed the lamp fixture, somebody's dirty works fell on her head.

One afternoon, Honey called me up from the theater, and said, "You've really got to come down here, they're showing an incredible film, *Desire for Men*." She was carrying on like it was Ingmar Bergman's debut. She said that the featured actress was a blonde named Long Jeanne Silver, a woman with a peg leg. I said I'd be right down.

My first revelation about porn movies was that they were, in fact, movies. I don't know why—all the hysteria about how bad they were, how dehumanizing—but it was genuinely a shock to me to see a full-length feature with real actors and real drama, sexual drama, unfolding before me. They weren't just bodies, they opened their mouths; and you could tell this one came from Queens, and this one was a surfer, and this one was a little brat, and this fellow was so full of himself it was almost endearing. Sometimes the director had the gods with him, and I actually got drawn into the little story or setup he was creating. Sometimes I could tell it was all they could do to get the sex act on film. But then when the sex did happen—cock entering cunt, tongue licking ass, faces all crazy when they came—my goodness, docudramas don't get any realer than this! The put-up-or-shut-up authenticity of it all was audacious, it was radical.

Another thing I could see about porn—and this has changed a lot since video took over—was that it was far less formulaic than

Hollywood or television in some ways. Long Jeanne Silver was only the beginning of an endless list of actresses who had every physical attribute under the sun. You can look like whatever you are and be a porn star.

Directors also had their little stamp; they were instantly recognizable, every one an auteur. They had this crass list of what kind of sex had to be in the film, but other than the "position" agenda, they were on their own voyage. Some directors had a social message they were determined to get in, along with the fucking and sucking. Some were clearly in love with one of the players, and built the film around their infatuation. Some thought they were producing the cinematic follow-up to *Sympathy for the Devil*. Others obviously had a wonderful time doing all that blow and dope, and just wanted to show you what a great party you had missed. Many porn directors are cinematographers who simply have an undying love affair with their lens. I'll never forget the time a close friend of mine in the business pointed out a porn film that I'd enjoyed tremendously called *3 AM*, and said of the director, "He was Orson Welles's cameraman for fifteen years." The same was true about Charles, my girlfriend's boss. He just loved to SEE with his camera—the human body, the night sky, the end of the world.

I was not consciously aroused the first time I went to a porn theater. For one thing, I was shocked by the quality; for another, I was terrified that one of the paying customers at the theater was going to molest me. I was once felt up by some jerk when I was fourteen, at a screening of *The Lady and the Tramp* that I attended by myself, so I just sort of multiplied the consequences of going from a Disney flick to a smut screen. At the very least, I feared that the seat I chose in the dark would inevitably turn out to be covered with cold, wet come. My girlfriend lent me a flashlight.

As it happens, the men in the theater were much more frightened of me than I was of them. They scattered from every row I approached; I began to see that their eyes held the frankly paranoid delusion that I had been sent by someone—their wife? their boss?—to spy on them. The most disgusting aspect of a porn theater is what an assembly of closet cases the audience is. Everyone is deadly quiet, except for the popcorn crunching and the breathing of those in the back getting blow jobs from their brethren. When something funny happened in the movie, which was quite common, I would laugh out loud—and completely alone. In all my time in porn theaters, strip joints, and peep shows—and believe me, I've logged as many hours as any raincoater you'll ever meet—I have only been spoken to, in a conversational way, two or three times. I have to hand it to the first guy who approached me—he got right to the point: "Why are you here?"

In the beginning, I wasn't sure why I was there. I was crazy about movies, and I thought porn had really gotten a raw deal, being so unwelcome in normal dinner table conversations. I was really in love with my girlfriend; I thought she was a genius and a great adventurer. And I was a feminist, working in a "feminist vibrator store" where we were so politically correct that we didn't carry anything that looked like a penis (at least not in front of the counter), and when our customers asked us about "erotica," we really didn't have a clue how to advise them. I felt it was my professional and political duty to find out what and where all the good dirty movies were.

But the other concern, in the back of my mind, was that I wondered if I was capable of being aroused by pictures, still or moving, of people in the act of sexual abandon. I had no experience of it. I certainly had been frightened by those kinky Polaroids I found when I was a child, and I had pawed through *Playboy*s I found at my father's house, but they were more like anatomy lessons to me, of cheesecake that I could admire or wonder about. They never made me reach down and touch myself.

Reading, on the other hand, reading sexy stories, was my very, very favorite way of getting off. I had mastered the art of holding a book and turning the pages with one hand while fingering my clit with the other. Those words on the page, the *Penthouse* letters in all their "needless to say" glory—just thinking about the font that those letters were set in makes me all creamy with nostalgia. I had my favorite fantasies, and when I saw them in print, it was like a direct line to my orgasm. I had never had that experience with living color photography.

Now my girlfriend had several jobs, one of them as the porn cashier and another as a banquet waitress working out of a union hiring hall. She was about the only woman working in a crew of the most unbelievable set of queens you'd ever hope to meet in the Tenderloin. One of her favorite work partners was named Victor—rest in peace, my friend—a Texas immigrant and totally devout Catholic who carried two books in his satchel: a leather-bound bible, and a paperback copy of a little classic called *How to Enlarge Your Penis*. Victor thought I was beautiful, he thought I had the figure of Marilyn Monroe. He gave me pearls for my birthday, and one day, after some outrageous fight he'd had with a lover, he decided to move all of his belongings into storage, and asked if I would like to "borrow" his big-screen TV/VCR.

Some of you may already know that the only reason we even have VCRs and big screens on the consumer marketplace is because porno fans demanded them and bought them in droves. I didn't know that in 1981; I didn't know anything except that if I put Victor's big screen in my bedroom, it only left about six inches to get out the door. It was enormous. When you lay in bed to look at the screen, you felt like you were going to be interrogated and swallowed. He left me a few videos, too—all "straight"—since, par for the course, Victor had no voyeuristic interest in watching gay male performances—only men with women.

The first movie I watched at home was some sort of sailboat orgy fiesta. I was excited before I even pressed the PLAY button, because I'd made sure no one was at home, and I felt altogether uninhibited—much more free and comfortable than in the Market Street movie palace.

I watched the couple on the sailboat giggle and take their clothes off, but I couldn't really make out any dialogue—Victor's audio system seemed to be hopelessly broken. "Mrwarrrr rahhdgh blehhh," went the girl who proffered her ass to the camera. This was getting annoying. I didn't feel the least bit attracted to anything. I poked the STOP button and felt like slapping somebody. Then I made a very important move, so dreamily and intuitively that I couldn't have told you where I thought it would lead. I plugged in my vibrator, put it in my lap, and pushed PLAY again. The same idiots frolicked under the sails; the camera moved close to the fat guy's cock; it was enormous, purple veins, the whole deal. Then we moved to the girl's behind, all plump and spanky, her hands reached behind to pull her cheeks apart, and she had a forest of dark hair running up her cunt to her ass. There were drops of something on her pussy hair, it was matted in places, wet. The camera and the stud moved closer to her, one of them expertly parted her thighs and lifted her a little with one hand, and right then, just with the tip, the purple cock slid in. My clit jumped like an alarm clock.

I never would have felt it if the vibrator hadn't been humming against me. You have to remember, above the neck I was watching this silly trash and saying, "What a piece of silly trash!" But when his cock touched her, the opening of her wet lips, the words flashed across my mind's eye—he's fucking her from behind—and I came like a bullet.

Well, of course, the first time is always a little bit special—I don't know if I've ever come to another porn film with as much force and speechless shock. I don't remember the name of the movie, which is so much like the anonymous heroism of porn—you never learn the name of the person who saves you. Many porn flicks later, I would find that I was a sucker for any sort of rear approach—don't even bother trying to figure it out, it's just another point of light in my thousands of irrational fantasies, but the first time was such an illumination. I had only succeeded in turning off my intellectual doubts and disdain by turning a Hitachi Magic Wand directly onto my clit. God, no wonder so many people are impervious to arguments about the value of pornography—clearly, it sometimes takes a physical intervention!

My confrontation with Victor's gigantic screen was the equivalent of Newton's apple: I began to connect the dots. I saw in my own body how inexplicable sensations could happen from seeing pictures that triggered my fantasies, and that I only relished these things when I felt uninhibited, without anyone watching or judging me. I could see how porn formulas were essentially a shotgun approach to hitting a number of broad sexual scenes, hoping that somewhere along the line the viewers would find where their erotic mind met a single frame—and voilà! That's the secret of the pause button and the instant replay.

What I perceived was the Pink Elephant of the pornography discussion: what turns you on may not match your artistic values, your romantic choices in real life, your political views, but it is just as much a part of you, just as real and substantial, as any other aspect. It's not a defect or a weakness, it's your intuitive ability to take all that's unbearable and crazy and unspeakable about life and turn it into juice—eroticism. Don't you dare go around with your nose in the air pretending that anybody's fantasies are low-class or despicable, because without that juice you wouldn't be alive, wouldn't be able to discriminate; you'd be a stranger both to your capacities and your limits.

Pornography is like four-letter words—an unaccepted language that exists in every tongue in the world, the first to be expressed and the first to be suppressed. Here's your world without porn—a world without sex, without creation. Expressing sex is always the first way we try to communicate, and it leaves its marks everywhere. Look at every technological innovation in communications, from cave drawing to the printing press to giant VCRs to the Internet.

The big bamboozle of pornography panics is that it's always treated like a defect, like something to vote yes or no on, instead of a natural expression of life. Eroticism's tenacious power—in the face of every single public leader speaking against it, every church, every worried parent—really gives you pause. This expression is not going anywhere, until talking, writing, filming, and showing sex becomes something the human appetite is oblivious to.

Critics of porn are not thrilled with human appetites, the whole notion that it's "natural" and therefore worthy. They might say, "Well, it's perfectly natural to feel like bopping people on the head, but what is the point in encouraging it?" What is the point in encouraging lust?

When I'm in my biological determinist mood, I feel like steering such people toward a few reruns of *Wild Kingdom* to see if they can get a grip on why sniffing and rutting and going into heat are all part of the big picture, and why we seem not only to do the sexual deeds, but to create an aesthetic for it.

But porn has been more of an inspiration to me than I could have guessed when I first accepted the dare to walk on its turf. I looked, criticized, gasped, and got my rocks off. But my interest went way beyond my hormones. Before I knew it, reading other people's sexual bodies became as revealing and mind-bending to my world as only the greatest works of art can be. Eventually, I had to roll my own—make my own erotic creations in print, with my crummy camera and my friends who believed as I did, that a pornographic sisterhood was potent stuff. We didn't know what we were doing, we hadn't one clue, but you know what? In the pornographic imagination, not knowing what you're doing gets awfully close to the truth.

As Porn as We Wanna Be

TEN YEARS AGO, I held an auction in my living room. It started out as a housecleaning crisis and turned into the most efficient way I could get rid of over 200 X-rated videos. I'd collected a surplus from my two years of work as an erotic movie reviewer, and I couldn't stand them cluttering up the house any longer.

"Let's give them away!" I suggested to my lover. "We can make an event out of it."

"Serve the People Porno," my invitation read. "You are part of a select clique of sympathetic pornophiles invited to help clear out my video surplus. Be prepared to be discriminating. We'll play you excerpts from all the tapes and provide dicey commentary to assist in your choices."

I divided the tapes up into categories: Amateur, Bimbo, Yuppie Couples, Gay, Interracial, Kinky, Spanish, Japanese, Star Vehicles, Auteur, and Transsexual. "Bimbo" was by far the largest group, and contained lightweight trash of both the male and female variety.

Our guests were purposefully pulled from every corner of our social life: couples, singles, straight, gay, suburban lawyers, Marxist diehards, and veteran dominatrixes, all nesting impatiently in front of my TV screen. Three of the women had never seen a porn film be-

155

fore. We gave everyone 100 points to use as bidding chips, and advised them to put their inhibitions aside.

The auction began. I showed random moments from each video, describing the high and low points. Our very first round knocked me for a loop. The clean and sober lesbians forced a bidding war over a John Holmes tape. The straight suburban couple put half their savings together on a gay S/M dungeon fantasy. The Marxists were collecting a mountain of cheap bimbo loops. My gay men friends provided insightful gossip on many of the "straight" actors.

Frantic trading and unbridled greed were the order of the day. But six hours later, as the guests trooped out the door, Safeway shopping bags full, I knew they meant it when they thanked me for an unforgettable experience.

When I first threw my porno pajama parties, I was filled with zeal to tell people the TRUTH about the pornographic film business. I relished the thought of their mouths dropping open as I dispelled the myths and clichés, revealing to them the reality—which is still pretty exciting and interesting stuff, even if it isn't an urban legend of horror, rape, and sadistic exploitation.

I took a version of my porno show on the road, and thought of myself as a one-woman campaign to stamp out erotic illiteracy. The days when only a doctor, lawyer, or politician on the stump had the right to comment on sexual matters was over. How could sex be the one subject that everyone has a personal history with, but no one feels qualified or courageous enough to speak about?

I was sure I had looked at enough dirty pictures to know what I was taking about, and I had no hesitation to go public with it. At first, I thought the main thing I'd confront was people asking, "Why isn't porn bad for you?" But the more I traveled around, the more I realized the big question was simply, "Why is porn so bad?" They weren't demanding explanations for morality, they wanted to know about the MEDIOCRITY. And even though everyone meant a little something different by "badness," it just seemed to be the porn genre's natural companion, like peanut butter and jelly.

One component of being bad is being made on the cheap. The porn industry makes movies with thousands of dollars, not millions, and they are shot in a matter of hours or days, not weeks or months. Porn is a satellite of the central film industry, operating its own camp just like the other B and C movie worlds of trailer trash horror, drive-in specialties, and badly dubbed Hong Kong action pictures.

Porn, in fact, follows on the heels of violence exploitation flicks as the wave of things to come to the mainstream. Certainly movies like *Striptease* and *Showgirls,* as stinky as they were to critical review, are evidence of the appetite to bring the sex business, and sex business heroines, into the forefront. Porn entertainers want to be visible, especially the new generation; and they have no apologies, only ambitions to keep tearing down the walls of criminality and stigma that keep porn in the twilight zone of movie distribution.

That twilight zone—of restricting or stigmatizing theaters, locations, and audiences—has been traditionally maintained by the ratings system, in particular the notorious X. It would be one thing if X simply meant no minors allowed, but in reality it has meant that no "decent" people should watch these movies, and no one who wants to make an influential picture should bother producing one. The MPAA ratings system, after decades of routing sex out of legitimate motion pictures, is thankfully falling apart, due to tremendous dissatisfaction on the part of audiences and artists. The notion of NC-17 is just the beginning. What we're actually seeing now is a two-tiered system of movies. If you're lucky enough to live in a big city, you can see the director's version of a movie with a sexual element to it, whereas if you're in shopping-mall land, you get the schoolkid treatment: no naughty sex parts allowed. Adult audiences aren't happy about it, they don't feel they should be condescended to just because they live in the suburbs.

Money, distribution limitations, censorship, all go a long way to explaining what makes a porn movie look "bad." But they don't entirely explain the absence of a reasonable script, or the performers we see who not only aren't acting, but seem to be ANTI-acting. I remember seeing an actress win an award at a Porn Oscars ceremony, and my first reaction was, How could she win?—she chews gum in every scene! Sure enough, she snapped her gum right up to the stage to collect her statuette. Everyone applauded wildly. That's when I began to get it—porn isn't just diabolically crummy—there's something we love about it that way.

When I think about my first porn pajama party, the tapes that riveted our attention most were either a few golden oldies from the seventies, that conveyed Hollywood proportions of style and substance—or, from the contemporary collection, the films where the performers seemed to be moving into our living room, taunting our voyeurism, upping the ante for how raw we could take it.

In the age of "adult video," we have two schools of porn making. First is the soap opera–style cable channel fare, which brings an *All My Children* feel to X-rated escapades. Its rude cousin is the so-called "amateur" school of porn, a group that despises plot and embraces autobiography, in all its tattered glory.

The movies you see in hotel rooms, or for sale with the glossiest packaging, are the soap-style. They are marketed as couples tapes, something for Jack and Jill. On the Jill end, what they seem to be selling is animated Victoria's Secret catalogs. The hair styling and costuming in the pornography business is every bit as good as in the fanciest Hollywood movie. The lingerie is flawless. It's a kind of look that appeals to a great many people; but I wonder about that look, frankly. Everyone from my aunt to my lesbian housecleaner has told me that they really like these movies, and I do believe people authentically enjoy them. However, I find these videos—with their refined portrayal of beautiful, wealthy, immaculate people having beautiful, wealthy, immaculate sex—don't arouse me as much as they send me a message: "Nice people have sex like this. Wealthy people suck and fuck. Really well-groomed, clean people have anal sex." The viewers get the immense reassurance of sitting down and watching a motion picture and saying, "See? I watched a pornographic movie. I wasn't offended. I'm not breaking out into hives. I'm perfectly fine. I'm intact."

These movies may or may not generate heat, depending on the individual performers, but the lacquered looks and vacuous plots of the product all promise respectability. It's the kind of respect you get for having a well-trimmed lawn, not for artistic achievement. I guess I'm so hard on them because I find keeping up with the Joneses to be anti-erotic, as well as anti-creative. My idea of a living hell would be having my sex life scripted like an episode of *General Hospital*. I like looking at beautiful bodies and faces as much as anyone, but the pretentiousness of the attitude seems more designed to save someone's face than to get turned onto it.

The rebellion to bourgeois porno has been the self-titled amateur explosion, a rebellion of the lewd, the crude, and the flip. They don't need your stinkin' cable, because they're marching to their own camcorder now. Amateur videos are the crystal ball of what you'll see duplicated in more refined pornography in the seasons to come. If a certain kind of sexual look or behavior is successful in the amateurs, you'll see it proliferate, and move into the soap opera lineup with higher-quality lingerie.

What is AMATEUR? It includes newcomers to video-making, but lots of professionals as well. When home cameras first became popular, there were swingers who made tapes of themselves and their lovers to trade with others, much like a Grateful Dead tape kind of phenomenon. Their scene was neither huge nor commercial, it was for dedicated wife and husband swappers who were using the latest technology to enhance their sex life. From there, a few enthusiasts got the bright idea to start selling their home tapes through mail order, and the response was remarkable.

The pros, the experienced filmmakers who make what are called "pro-am" tapes, embraced this one-man studio philosophy and the bare-bones budget. These are the type of guys who could make a lovely, glossy video if they wanted to, but they don't. They are deliberately not cleaning up the bedroom, softening the lens—they are producing a more lived-in, streetwise look, and using performers who are as cinematically inexperienced and spontaneous as possible.

The rules for what sexual behavior can be shown in amateur videos are a lot looser. There's emphasis, for example, on showing women's orgasms. Their arousal and orgasm can be less than perfect—maybe they have hair in their face, maybe it's kind of a mess—but they're coming and you can tell. Or you can see that they're almost coming and they're frustrated—you can hear the huffing and puffing, the natural disarray that accompanies live sex. Amateur videos made by men, which means 90 percent of the field, are also filled with low-brow humor, which seems to be their brand of politics, à la Larry Flynt. The narrator, or the guy who gets fucked or at least holds the camera, often characterizes himself as a horny Bozo— a guy who can't get laid, won't give up, and miraculously scores in his obsessive efforts. You won't see these male characters in a cable-style porn tape, which is desperately trying to distance itself from white trash and working-class manners.

The amateur video is a hotbed of equal opportunity. You can have many surplus pounds and forty pimples on your butt, and still be an amateur porn star. Every age, race, and body type is exploited; the thrill is in the realness of the humanity presented. Amateur porn in this sense is like the current literary craze for memoirs instead of novels. Personal Truth is respected, and you can prove your honesty and individuality more by being flawed and a little tacky than by covering it up with a third-person story or nice makeup.

Amateur porn has not only changed the face and butt of who a superstar might be, but it has also taken the lead in demonstrating the sex that people want to see. Take anal sex, which has gone from being a specialty act in mainstream X-rated tapes to the focus of virtually every movie that is made. Even when the camera is not filming an anal penetration, you will see a focus on the woman's anus and ass in the course of regular intercourse. That's the direct result of amateur video, which never held back its fascination with anal sex, and could care less about—even relished—its homoerotic or S/M implications.

Now amateur is tackling one of the biggest taboos in old-school heterosexual porn: men bottoming to women's cocks. In amateur, we now see men getting fucked, completely in a heterosexual context. There's a whole series devoted to this subject on my video shelf: *Sam Gets the Shaft, Volume I, II, III*, etc. Sam, or whoever, will entertain some beautiful babe with a strap-on, and we see him get aroused at the same time she is being very feminine and simultaneously very aggressive.

When I was first involved in making lesbian-made porn videos (*Private Pleasures, Clips, Suburban Dykes*), somebody I met in the mainstream business said, "Oh, you're part of this emerging amateur trend." And I didn't know what they were talking about. Sure, I knew that my friends and I were amateurs—we really were, we didn't know what we were doing. In the first movie we made, the camera woman cried in the middle of shooting a scene: "There's no sound. I'm not getting any sound."

Our reaction? "Oh, well, we'll just put it out without any sound." We thought the women making love in front of us were so hot we didn't want to stop. We were doing something unheard of: lesbians making porn for their own desires and aesthetics, and that promise was enough for us to start rolling. We had to incorporate a lesbian fist-fucking scene if only to challenge the world. I suppose we were the punk girl accessory to the amateur wave.

We were not doing these movies to enhance our love lives, nor were we in some kind of lesbian swingers scene. We made our videos in a furious reaction to the mainstream feminist community, which treated lesbian sex like a nonentity—or believed we only performed polite, equal opportunity, five-minute cunnilingus kind of things with each other. Because we thought of ourselves as the counterculture, we didn't identify with the swingers or pro/amateur culture that was growing around the country—not until we realized that they were part of the audience too, as feverish as any of our dyke enclave. I didn't realize for at least two years that we were part of something much bigger: a do-your-own, roll-your-own school of erotic video-making where self-revelation, warts and all, was the highest calling.

The women's lesbian underground tapes that were genuinely amateur do have one thing in common with so-called amateur video, in that they're both grassroots operations. Both groups were made up of people who didn't have a lot of money, but had a lot of excitement about doing their own thing on camera. They didn't want to have to go through the regular rigmarole and porno bureaucracy to make their statement; they really believed there was an audience for something different, and there is.

The triumph of amateur porn and its penchant for bare ass and polysexual realism is that it has been the first explicit canvas that NON-erotic celebrities have exploited for themselves.

Famous athletes and courtroom defendants have moved into prime-time pornographic amateur hour. Al Capone could never have dreamed of this, but O.J. may have to soon. Witness the revolutionary debuts of castration victim John Wayne Bobbitt and award-winning figure skater/conspirator Tonya Harding into the hardcore field.

With Bobbitt's video, we have a man who made a sex tape not only for the money but also because he wanted absolute control over his story—and the porn people were the ONLY ones who would give him that. (Of course, since porn in today's legal climate can't portray "violence," when the movie arrives at the point where Lorena cuts his penis off, it just fades out.)

What we do see is John Wayne in the fashion he sees himself, and what he wants America to think he is. He could not have cut this deal with Hollywood or mainstream television, but he could with pornography. We find out the salient facts such as, yes, his penis seems to function. However, he cannot give head to save his life. He was so inept at cunnilingus, I couldn't believe he wasn't coached. He thinks he's solved his penis problem, but his tongue problems have only just begun. It put a whole different light on his problems with women.

As far as Tonya Harding goes, I'm one of these girls who grew up watching Peggy Fleming and Dorothy Hamill at the Olympics, the perfect ice princesses. I believed the last virgins-belles in America were figure skaters. All that has been put behind me now. In her wedding night keepsake video, Tonya Harding waves her big puffy wedding gown up in the air, gives a squeal, and flashes her G-string. Then even that is peeled off and she's sucking her husband's dick and Giloolly is going down on her. You see those same incredible muscles she displayed on the ice.

Tonya's honeymoon tape is one of the most classic pornographic experiences I've ever had. I felt so prurient watching it, because it seemed like something private that I shouldn't have been seeing. But they obviously wanted it to be seen, there was no fraud involved. These two were showing off for each other on their wedding night, and now for all of America to purchase at Big Top Video. I couldn't say, "I will pass this by because the very idea offends me"—I had to see it because Tonya is a sexually compelling figure to me, and I have been warped by the double standard of ice-skating erotic denial for years.

I think it's no coincidence that a world-class athlete would be one of the first to cross over into porn: Tonya on video, and to another degree, Dennis Rodman in his explicit memoirs, written at the height of his career. Porn stars are athletes, make no mistake; they drive themselves to physical perfection and endurance for success, believe in "No pain, no gain," and find a very early and ego-bruising end to what are predetermined youthful careers. Porn stars just wish they made the money and engaged the respect of their sport field colleagues. They certainly have the lifelong fans and the memories.

Athletes, and athlete life stories, on the other hand, are models for the structure of the typical amateur porn vehicle, where the performers put their humble beginnings on the table, and give it all they've got. No apologies for being poor or working class or uneducated; in fact, there's a pride to it, a pride in knowing that one's body, determination, and sheer physical charisma are WORTH something, that this authentic display will prove, or make points.

When people say that so much porn is bad, we really have to ask, well, how bad do you want it to be? And how bad do you want it, period? If we want porn with high production values, method acting, and sparkling scripts, then we need to scrap the existing laws against porn, and allow independent filmmakers to find their audience in whatever venue they want.

If we also want movies that capture the bare-bulb heat of realism and self-expression, orgasm-style, then we need to pay our respect to the "amateurs," and make a little confession that they are after all a voice of America's sexuality, not a rude aberration. My biggest gripe about the amateurs isn't the "bad" sound, "bad" clothes, or "bad" jokes—it's that since we've seen what straight and gay men and lesbians can do, it's about time for a little straight-girl amateur action. Now THAT would call for another historic pajama party.

On
the
Road

Talking in the Dark

SO WHAT IF I DIDN'T GO to the senior prom? I was "Miss Condom Congeniality" for two years running at U. C. Berkeley, and I've been rushed by more disaffected sorority sisters than you can shake a pair of Ben Wa balls at. Over the past decade, I've been invited to speak at campuses around the country on topics such as safe sex, pornography, and the sexual state of the union—much to the consternation of the homophobic right wing and the sexophobic left wing, and the delight of every inhibition-weary undergraduate.

"I just can't believe I'm hearing the word *pussy* on a University of Arkansas podium," said a student particularly moved by my lecture. I can't believe I'm saying various p-words either, at colleges from the Ivy League to the Pac-10. What's going on? I call it "Revenge of the Coeds." Students know that they're at the heart of every morality and sex-prevention speech on television, pulpit, and congressional floor, and they are determined to have their say in public as well.

I am usually invited, and then received, by a sympathetic crowd that wants to crack open the uncomfortable silences about sex, and hopes I will lead the way. However, in some schools, I represent a controversial perspective in the campus's feminist corridors. In fact, the reaction is so unpredictable that I can never tell whether I'm going to get a commencement speaker invitation (University of California), incite a bomb threat (Wellesley), or confront a manifesto accusing me of being the next atrocity in line after the Holocaust (University of Minnesota).

In between smelling the bouquets and being interviewed by the bomb squad, I received one special invitation in late 1993 to speak at a campus that had recently captured the nation's headlines by declaring a student-initiated sexual behavior policy: Antioch College, Ohio.

ANTIOCH SEXUAL OFFENSE POLICIES

All sexual contact and conduct on the Antioch College campus and/or occurring with an Antioch community member must be consensual. Obtaining consent is an ongoing process in any sexual interaction. Verbal consent should be obtained with each new level of physical and/or sexual contact/conduct in any given interaction, regardless of who initiates it. Asking "Do you want to have sex with me?" is not enough. The request for consent must be specified to each act.

Clearly such a policy is a tall order, but it comes with the pioneering traditions of the Antioch community. Antioch is one of the most left-wing, innovative universities in the country, located in a tiny town in southern Ohio. There are only 600 students on campus, and 70 percent are female. To fulfill the school's philosophical mandate, students are required to complete an internship in the field they seek to research. Practically speaking, this means that for half the year, undergraduates are required to work a job—any job, from removing asbestos from buildings, to stripping in New Orleans, to advising Clinton—and then turn in papers on their experiences.

I arrived on campus to give a talk the night of Antioch's winter break holiday, which kicks off with the biggest student party of the year. I was told nonchalantly that the basic recipe for the party is for everyone to get drunk, perhaps add psychedelics, and then get laid, followed the next morning by hangover appearances in the "Hall of Shame" (the cafeteria), where no one is able to look in the eye of the individual they screwed the night before.

Now does this sound like a place where the average student—or any student—is living by the decree of the new sexual offense policy? NO! Indeed, Antioch students are proud of their policy; it's a very important piece of window-dressing to them, and they resent the press or any outsider criticizing how they run their school. They are scornful of critics who dislike their emphasis on the verbal articulation of consensus at each step of sexual interplay. Nevertheless, if they feel you are a friend or sympathetic to their aims, they're the first to tell you that this policy has NOTHING to do with their personal sex lives, and in fact they can't think of anyone who adheres to it. It's as if the policy exists to punish outsiders exclusively. Meanwhile, everyone on campus is having sex as usual, dispensing with the "simultaneous mutual consensus" part.

It's important to recognize that the policy is not based on any grassroots development in sexual relations between students. It was drafted by baby Dworkin-ites, those inhabiting the puritan wing of the women's movement, who graduated long before they ever saw their guidelines adopted and adapted by the administration. However, their intellectual heirs are still around, and a hot and bothered group of them organized a vocal protest at my speech, calling me to task for all the women and children I've tortured, mutilated, and murdered in my pornographic career. They were convinced ahead of time that I was a plague upon all womanhood.

Before I spoke, the most articulate of the undergrad antiporn organizers went around to all the lunch tables in the cafeteria (this is how you get things done on a small campus!) and told everyone that

I was going to "attract disturbed and perverted men" to the campus who would try to assault the women after my lecture concluded. Of course, some people came to my talk just to see if that horrible scenario would play out, but I'm afraid they were disappointed. My "normal" appearance and manner must have disappointed everyone waiting for a super-dominatrix to appear with slaves in tow; but no matter how I looked or what I said, the Stop-Susie crowd was clearly displeased with me from start to finish.

I could tell stories about each of the women who was afraid of or angry at me. They were certainly not all dykes. Some were pretty, some plain. One of them bragged that she and her mother had spent their summer vacation dropping leaflets protesting sadomasochism from a helicopter over the Michigan Women's Music Festival—a mother-daughter anti-kinky brigade! Another student, anxious to thwart my pro-sex comments, got up in the middle of my talk to yell, "Women who are raped have orgasms too!" Oh, that's helpful. Does that mean that orgasm leads to rape, or that this is the sort of thing one can EXPECT from having orgasms? One young man got up and said hopefully, "I'd like to talk about male passion—if I could." I tried to imagine what a Permission Slip for male passion would be like. (The only other male I heard from was the self-proclaimed leader of a libertarian group on campus who wanted to know if I "believed in incest." Is that anything like believing in Santa Claus?)

I think the students' more earnest criticism comes from the belief that they think I place hedonism above social equality—you know, I don't care how many dead bodies I have to climb over to get my little orgasm! What annoyed me was the way they set up this either/or choice: social principles versus sexual pleasure. They have screwed up so much anger that they think they can give up free speech in return for social equality—and be happy with the deal. To me, that's like saying, "You can have your bread or your water, but you can't have both." My position, meanwhile, is that one can strive against

bigotry and oppression but still acknowledge that one has an unconscious life, a fantasy life, a creative life that does not function like a
bureaucracy.

One trembling girl stood up after my talk to attack what she believed was my defense of the "white male beauty myth." With tears
in her eyes, she said, "It's a beauty myth that stands for the thin, the
blonde, the blemish-free." She was a very slim, fair girl with long yellow hair, and her face was covered with pimples. Was her speech
truly about the cruelties of femininity, or did this have to do with being eighteen years old and wondering if anybody is ever going to desire her? I thought to myself, "You're attending a tiny school where
all the boys are dorky and immature, and you want someone wonderful to love you, someone who thinks you're beautiful." Now
could I say that out loud without humiliating her? No. So I didn't.
But it's the truth.

All the so-called "feminist politics" these students referred to
come directly from a feminist sex debate that is seventeen years old.
They were in diapers when I was first arguing over these issues myself, and they are only now in the midst of discussions that were
shelved years ago in New York and San Francisco. The women's
studies department at Antioch—and bless their hearts if they've re-
formed since I wrote this chapter—has made a bonfire over my
philosophies. Sometimes a given women's studies program will be divided about the subject of women's sexual agency and the battle to
expand, expunge, or defend pornography, but the most evolved have
reached a point where they realize there are no "illegitimate" positions. Unfortunately, I'd reached the outpost where I was still a
bastard.

The Antioch sexual offense policy does reflect a certain dated era
in the feminist discussion of sex, but at this point, it's as much about
the isolation of a small town in the Midwest as it is about anything.
Despite its gender-neutral language, the policy is interpreted as a

threat to naughty boys, and a bossy stick for girls. The policy seems doomed to be used vindictively, if at all, because it has nothing to do with ordinary campus life. When I visited Antioch, no one could imagine such a possibility; but look a little more closely. On the surface, the policy itself seems right-minded in terms of clarifying the notion of consensuality; but the people who created it, and who will enforce the sexual offense procedures, are ruthless in both their morality and their undisguised sexual repression.

Meanwhile, various students are having LSD and beer busts in their dorm rooms, playing rock and roll, and contemplating how to set up the next party. After my lecture, I went to a bash in the student union where they were playing loud hip hop, smoking homegrown, and sure enough, everyone started kissing and rubbing up against each other. Forget about asking anyone's consent; you couldn't hear a bloody thing above the music. The women who were concerned about my bad influence did not attend this party. I asked the dyke who was my party chaperone, "What about the step-by-step guidelines?" And she said, "Are you kidding? We don't even know who we'll be TALKING to in the dark."

Coed Confidential

I KNEW I WAS getting old when one year I went on my annual speaking pilgrimage to various universities, looked out at the crowd, and imagined what my daughter would be like at that age. When I first started teaching on campuses, I was of undergraduate age myself: those students were the same age as my peers and lovers, and I knew that many of the same things were going through our minds. I certainly didn't have people asking me petrified-fossil questions like the girl who raised her hand at one of my last lectures and said, "So what is it like to get it on when you're thirty-seven?"

"Well, first I bend over my walker, and then . . ."

Typically I am invited to these college gigs because of "AIDS awareness." The colleges are dedicated to educating their students on how to protect or conserve themselves, and they will put up good money for some expert to come in and spell out the do's and don'ts. I'm qualified as such an expert, thus the invitation, but I have no intention of showing my audience how to put a condom on a banana. I know they've already been inundated with safe-sex packages and speeches, and while it's very interesting to find out whether they in fact put any of this stuff into practice, I'm not going to patronize them with another "Beware Young'uns" lecture. I know when I appear in front of a college group that I am addressing some people who have never had sex before and feel like the biggest geeks on earth, and some people who are having their sexual premieres and wondering in disappointment, "Is that all there is?" Some of these students are having secret affairs that their parents would kill them for because it's with the "wrong" type of person; others are about to come out of the closet with their true sexual preference; some are gloriously in love and feel truly sexy for the first time in their lives. It's all those first times, first sensations, first doubts—my God, it's like going off to the moon. Talking about "safe sex techniques" is secondary to dealing with the main event, which is their brand spanking new sexual identity.

As outrageous as some of the students' questions can be, it's their lack of self-consciousness that keeps me coming back for more. They will tell me more about their sex lives and erotic dilemmas than any group ten years older would. They think that sex matters, politically and personally; in fact, it's one of the only things they think matters, so we're on similar tracks there. Youth culture is interested in the authentic essentials: bodily fluids, sex, death, things that can be demonstrated. They like over-the-top declarations of love and passion and dedication; they know everybody is a star, it's just all so fleeting.

The students who come to my lectures aren't necessarily sympathetic or knowledgeable about me—they do tend to be bored, and totally cynical about the usual kind of sex ed. they see on campus—and therefore willing to check me out just in case I accidentally let loose some half-truth kernel of sexual wisdom, or amusingly make an ass of myself.

The last round of schools I visited were all private schools on the East Coast, largely liberal arts—small enough that probably everyone would know everyone else in the room. Since that can be a little intimidating for freewheeling discussion, I decided that for maximum discussion of the issues at hand, I should devise an essential sex survey—something quick, dirty, and anonymous. As soon as the students entered the auditorium, I handed each a white index card and a pencil. I explained that as much as I wanted to talk to them about the wide world of sexual politics, it would be helpful to understand exactly where they were coming from first.

My queries were all designed to tell the most basic things about their sexual lives. The first question was, "Do you masturbate?" I explained that this was a two-parter: "Do you do it at all? If so, is it a pleasurable activity?" The second question followed immediately from the first: "Do you have orgasms? And do you enjoy having orgasms?"

The boys in the room burst out laughing at both queries. The girls looked at them indignantly. The boys take masturbation and orgasm for granted, but for the women, this is a do-or-die question! The young women knew that already, but it had never occurred to the men that this was the biggest gender gap of all. So often, on the cards I got back, the women would write next to the orgasm question a YES!!! with exclamation marks, like it was a tremendous accomplishment—no boy did that. Many women questioned whether they had an orgasm or not—they weren't sure—but every man was certain one way or the other. Some women answered "No" to masturbation, but said that they did have orgasms, but only with a partner, which meant they were dependent on that partner to come. None of the men shared that experience.

Next I asked if they had ever had sex with another person, and I was surprised how many had. Maybe the Chastity Club was boycotting me, or those Gallup polls are really off the mark. Or perhaps I got a more inclusive response because I don't make the usual assumptions about "intercourse": I made sure to say that "sex" didn't have to be penis-vagina intercourse, but the participants had to feel they had experienced a substantial, complete-feeling sexual encounter with another human being.

Then I asked them if they were attracted to men, women, or both—deliberately not using orientation labels like *gay* or *bi*, since they are potentially meaningless when it comes to someone's personal behavior. The gay statistics were pretty typical (8 percent for men, 12 percent for women), but what really interested me was the "both" statistics: 29 percent for the guys, 43 percent for the girls. In their comments, they would often say that they hadn't actually had an experience with the same sex, but that they thought about it, fantasized about it, or liked to keep an open mind. Some of them felt it was impossible to eliminate an entire gender from their sexual possibilities, as if swearing off half the planet.

I thought it was interesting that only 64 percent of the men identified themselves as straight, period. I don't think I would have gotten that result when *I* was in college; men were much more uptight about bisexuality. No men answered "not sure," but some women did, indicating again that women are less confident in general about what turns them on.

My last question was, "How's your love life?" If they had to rate their overall sex life these days on a scale from one to ten, where would it fall? I added that I knew this exercise was terribly unfair, to be assigning a number that might change next week, but I just wanted a spur-of-the moment temperature reading on their sexual happiness.

This was the one question that the women were much more affirmative about: 50 percent of them rated their sex life from seven to ten, compared to 36 percent of the guys. I gathered from the men's comments that they were answering this question from the point of view of "Am I getting any?" But for many of the women, it wasn't a question of whether they were HAVING sex—it was a question of how SATISFYING it was. Some women who were partnered gave themselves a low mark because they were so disillusioned with the quality, and of course some women were simply single and miserable. There were a few men and women who gave themselves a ZERO, even though my scale started at one.

Averages of Student Sex Surveys

Responses from 351 women and 111 men at Williams, Bryn Mawr, Vassar, and Wesleyan Colleges:

DO YOU MASTURBATE: DO YOU HAVE ORGASMS?

4% of the men do not masturbate or do not enjoy masturbating; 98.6% of the men are orgasmic.

18% of the women do not masturbate or do not enjoy masturbating; 13.3% of the women are not orgasmic or do not know if they have had an orgasm.

HAVE YOU HAD SEX WITH ANOTHER PERSON?

7.6% of the men have not had sex with other people; 2% report "yes, but" (indicating nonconsensual or questionable).

15% of the women have not had sex with other people; 1% report "yes, but."

ARE YOU ATTRACTED TO MEN OR WOMEN OR BOTH?

8% of the men identify as being attracted to men, 64% to women, 29% to both.

45% of the women identify as being attracted to men, 12.3% to women, 43% to both, 2% reported that they don't know.

How would you rate your sex life these days, from 1–10?

Men who chose 0–3:	24.6%
Men who chose 4–6:	39%
Men who chose 7–10:	36%
Women who chose 0–3:	28.3%
Women who chose 4–6:	27.6%
Women who chose 7–10:	50.6%

Is There Good Sex After Vassar? . . .
And Other Student
Sex Questions

AT THE BOTTOM OF their cards, I asked my undergraduate guinea pigs to write down any question about sex they had on their minds: personal, political, anatomical, whatever. When they turned in the cards, I picked a few at random to read. Everyone was on pins and needles, hoping I would choose their anonymous offering, or at least one that sounded like theirs. The questions were fantastic and prompted me to suggest having a sexuality forum on campus, where these things would get addressed in as frank a manner as they deserve.

Though the one-of-a-kind questions were as pertinent as the common ones, I couldn't help but speculate about the concerns that came up over and over. Erotic compatibility was a big one—trying to find someone who liked you the way you liked them, would touch you the way you wanted to be touched, let you touch them the way you fantasized it could be. Everyone seemed to agree—feeling on a different wavelength from your partner is a rotten place to be. Searching for a partner, period, was on a lot of people's minds: the whole question of how to even get to page one, how to test the waters, how to be intuitive.

As for the technique questions, the number one thing men asked was how to perform cunnilingus and do it "right." On the girl side, the overwhelming questions about sexual performance were: "How can I come? How can I come more easily? How can I come at all?" Even though only 13 percent of the women polled said they had never experienced orgasm, from the questions it seemed like half the women in the crowd were orgasmically frustrated one way or another. Yikes! Talk about sublimated anger. Now is there a correlation between guys wanting to know how to give a woman head and women who aren't getting off? I think the men who were asking were doing so not just to collect data, but because they want to please a woman; I mean, if they were crazy about eating pussy for their own sake, they would have figured it out by now, because enthusiasm is 80 percent of the trick. So clearly, the men asking want to know because they think it is a valuable lovemaking ability, one for which they want to be appreciated. (My friend Ari, who I turned to for his spontaneous guy-on-the-street opinion, doesn't share my optimism—he insists that guys just want to know how things work for the hell of it, like how to wind an antique cuckoo clock. I pray that their interest isn't so purely mechanical.)

While men were searching for clit, women were asking where their G-spots were, and how they could ejaculate. It is such a female sex question, to be searching for your sex: WHERE IS IT, WHERE IS IT? Men don't have this location problem.

Not surprisingly, the most common questions that were not performance-oriented had to do with fantasy: erotic wishes and daydreams. So many people asked, "What does it mean if I think about lesbian sex but I've never done it?" or confessed, "I think about being called nasty names in bed" or, "I think about getting it on with more than one person." The unspectacular but right-on analysis of these thoughts is that THINKING them is what really turns the person on. Some may just be on their way to fulfilling some of these fantasies, while others will linger in their dream worlds, bold and unswerving, without ever making the slightest effort to realize them. Our culture's obsessive belief that every wish, every image is as fleshy as the deed itself is a total crock, at odds with everything we understand about our unconscious. We take this point for granted in some instances—like when we imagine boiling our calculus teacher in oil, or burning down the student loan department; no one would think twice if we were to utter these terrible threats and fantasies.

Young people carry a special burden with regard to their fantasies, because so often their sexual lives are just beginning, whereas their fantasy lives have been alive and kicking since they were little. So many things are finally available to them that they can be really confused between what is firmly on their agenda and what they'd prefer to keep playing out only in their minds. For example, there was a time when I was very curious about vibrators and I wanted to try one, and I knew all I had to do was walk a block from my house and go to the vibrator store; however, in retrospect, I wouldn't say it was an erotic fantasy of mine. Vibrators themselves never appear in my fantasies—they're just not an erotic object to me. I remember fantasizing about anal sex before I'd ever done it, and when I did try it for the first time, it was awkward and it hurt and I felt ridiculous; nevertheless, that event had absolutely NO effect on the graceful, hot, totally zipless buttfuck fantasy that persisted in my mind.

What was so impressive about these undergrad questions was that they were so "grown up" compared to the image the mainstream media gives of college kids' natural sexual sensitivity—which is that they're all innocent babes and/or total heathens. The questions that my audience posed were exactly the same ones that people in their thirties, forties, fifties, and sixties also ask.

My favorite part of the sex surveys I collect is reading the questions people ask. The value to me is to find out why these questions are so taboo. Why aren't they addressed as we grow up, become adult, become sexual with others? By the time kids get to college, they all know about the birds and the bees and all the nasty diseases you can get from having sex. But that's not all there is to sex, is it? Not by a long shot.

Teenagers and adults need to have forums to learn about sex, to understand how their bodies respond and function sexually, and how we arrive at our sexual customs. Sex educators need to be able to teach about sex, not horror stories about how you die from it, or the disembodied egg-sperm scenarios. No other subject so close to our lives is presented with so many outstanding gaps. We need to stop the hysterical notions that comprehensive sex education will create an army of nymphomaniacs, because what it WILL do is save a lot of lives and fearful minds. Even the most chaste human beings deserve to know about eroticism and sexuality, regardless of whether they're going to have a personal G-spot exploration tomorrow. Young people going through puberty, in particular, deserve to know how and why their bodies are changing so rapidly, and why everyone seems to want to have sex so bad when all they tell you in school is that it's bad for you! If sex—and sexual desire—has a positive side, a wonder of possibilities, then what are schools and parents accomplishing by suppressing that knowledge?

I read an editorial by critic Anne Roiphe last year in which she wrote that teenagers have sex for all sorts of sad and rebellious reasons. What I couldn't believe was that she left out the other half—the ecstasy and happiness of first sexual adventures, the intense comfort and familiarity that comes with finding your first lover, the first person you get to know intimately.

When I first became sexual, I had a yellow writing pad that I kept as a coded diary of my sex partners. I would write down their names, how old I was, how old they were, and for the first year I kept track of whether I had an orgasm or not, since that was both very significant to me and also something that felt entirely out of my hands. In Sex Year Number Two, I figured out that my orgasm was in my hands, literally, and I finally had enough confidence to show what I knew—and wanted—to anyone I went to bed with. So the orgasm code fell off my diary entries.

But the enduring controversy of my list was that, besides my hard-earned orgasms, I had to decide and record whether I was "in love" with these people—something which, I felt at the time, could be answered after one fuck. I think I started out with a star symbol, which meant this was L-O-V-E. But then the next person I slept with, oh, I loved him so much more, which made a mockery of my first star, so I decided on a two-star system. Well, four stars later, I was disgusted by my early recording scheme. How could I be so dense as to think those first lovers were my heart's desire?

By the end of my seventeenth year, I started to differentiate among erotic chemistry, friendship, whirlwind romance, infatuation, and just another profound acid trip. I know some people have a first love—the love of their life—early on, but for me it was a maturing thing. I've never loved anyone as deeply and unselfishly as I love now, and if I had met my current lover ten or twenty years ago, I'm sure my love and trust would not have been as complete. I will always relish the fire of my four-star lovers; they taught me what it was like to feel sexually alive, and at seventeen, that's a gift.

I stopped keeping a list of lovers when I experienced my first heartbreak, the night all the stars went out, the year I cried all the time. I even took a lover who was also heartbroken—it was the only way I could stand to share a bed; we could hold each other's open parts like the wounded little babies that we were. We would cry in bed together over the lost loves, and even share the horrible letters and postcards we'd last received from them.

I would have cold-cocked you if you had interrupted my heartbroken year and told me I was being "sad and rebellious." I was eighteen and I knew what desire was all about; I knew how to ache all over for all the best reasons and all the worst reasons. I think about this every time I speak to another group of young people today. Today's age-deprived are not so different from me in the early days: making lists with stars next to the names and waiting for the real thing—orgasmic bliss and true love.

Questions from Students

Bold-faced questions are from **men**; *italicized* ones are from *women*.

1. TECHNIQUE

Is there any way to make sure that (vaginal) fisting will work?
How can you have anal sex without having it hurt?
What about having anal sex with a man with him as a receiver?
What's the best position for women to have an orgasm during heterosexual sex?
Do all women get pleasure from having their breasts touched?
Why are men so clueless about female anatomy?
What are you supposed to do when you have oral sex?
What is the correct way to perform cunnilingus?
How can you learn to accommodate fisting?
How can you please a woman without having oral sex?
What is the secret of an expert blowjob?
Is it possible to have sex in a stand-up shower?
What are good tips for cunnilingus (besides being gentle)?
How can I last longer during sex?
How can I control my ejaculations during sex without breaking the natural flow of the experience?
How can I last longer?

How can you best give a woman oral sex?
What sexual positions would you recommend?
How do you perform great oral sex on a woman?
I can't have an orgasm with manual masturbation, only by friction—things like being on top during sex. How can I learn to masturbate manually?
Can you recommend a good natural lubricant for those dry days? The stuff at the store is too expensive and I like to use and make my own cosmetics.
How do you make safe sex unclinical?
I want advice on kissing.
How on earth are you supposed to perform sex with a dental dam?
What are the basic techniques males should know about cunnilingus?
Give me some concrete advice to help my girlfriend achieve orgasm.
What's the best way to improve a male's endurance?
Shouldn't guys know the essentials of a good blowjob—how to give a good one?

2. PSYCHOLOGICAL

What am I doing here?
Why do I like to be demanding during sex?
Is sexuality an important defining characteristic of individuals?
What do men look for in other men?
What do you think a speak-out on sexual pleasure would look like?
Why is there never enough time for sex?

3. PHYSIOLOGICAL

Is there really a G-spot? Does every woman have one? Am I broken for life?
What's up with the "wandering" clitoris? I've heard it moves location, like from side to side.

What do women like best about intercourse?

Please talk about female ejaculation. Am I ejaculating, or am I urinating, or something else weird?

What do you think of the G-spot?

How do females ejaculate?

What can you do if you want to like penetration, but aren't comfortable physically (i.e., can't even use tampons)?

What do you know about female ejaculation? (I ejaculate copiously and find it somewhat embarrassing, since I know so little about it.)

Where is the G-spot? I'm confused.

Is it possible to numb your clitoris with too much sex?

Do all women have G-spots?

Is there such a thing as too much sex?

Can you really get your entire forearm up your butt? Sounds scary . . .

I know where my clit is but it doesn't seem to work. Help!

Where IS your clitoris?

Does anal sex loosen your bum up and cause . . . problems?

Is anal sex actually more pleasurable for males than females?

4. ORGASM

What about if you can only come one way, the same way every time? ARGH!

What are all the different types of orgasms women can have and is there a spiritual women's sexual pinnacle?

Is having an orgasm while having sex with another person different from an orgasm from masturbation?

Can every woman have multiple orgasms? If so, how can I have them?

Why do I only orgasm when I masturbate and not when I have sex? Do all women have vaginal orgasms?

How do I know when I get an orgasm? Is it wrong if I've never really masturbated?

I have orgasms alone, but I can't with my boyfriend . . . any tips on how to relax? Also, my boyfriend has started to come a few minutes after we start sex. Help!

How can I make myself come?

How do you know if you've had an orgasm?

I haven't had an orgasm yet when making love with my boyfriend, and I'm sick of it!

How can one reach orgasm faster?

Do you have to have an orgasm to enjoy sex?

Since I haven't orgasmed, is it something that will change—and how?

Is there a difference between clitoral and vaginal orgasms?

How do you know you're having an orgasm?

I can't let myself have an orgasm. It sucks. Any suggestions?

How can I make orgasm easier?

Do women have to wait until they're older to have an orgasm?

What does an orgasm feel like?

How do women have a vaginal orgasm if they've only ever had a clitoral one?

I can't give myself an orgasm. Why?

How can I orgasm more?

Why can't I have an orgasm sometimes when I'm really turned on?

How can I orgasm more easily during sex?

Why don't I orgasm with other people?

Don't men and women have different orgasms?

What exactly does an orgasm feel like?

If you're used to using a vibrator and can't have an orgasm with someone else, what do you do?

What are multiple orgasms exactly? How many women can have one, and where can I get one?

What's the difference between clitoral and internal orgasm? Is there a difference?

What should you do if your partner can't come?

How many women don't have orgasm and what can they do about it?

I only have orgasms during sex (with another person). Does this mean it isn't possible any other way?

Is there any way to reach orgasm faster? When I'm with someone else it can take an hour. How can I best help my partner get me off, or reach orgasm faster?

I want to orgasm during sex, but how?

Why is it sometimes harder and takes longer for a woman to become horny and achieve orgasm right after waking up?

5. SEXUAL ORIENTATION

Do you ever feel less queer because you have long hair? I do.

Is it really different having sex with girls instead of boys?

How do I meet hot women if I have a very visible boyfriend?

You said that bisexuality is trendy but you like both sexes. Do you think that there really are 50/50 bisexuals or that everyone is?

When you say "Who do you like?" you should specify "like." I like women, and am attracted to them, but as of yet not physically.

How do you know if you're gay?

Why is there such a taboo about being attracted to people of both sexes?

How best to come out?

What's different about having sex with women as opposed to men?

How do you move from sleeping with men to sleeping with women?

Why would you sleep with men after being a lesbian?

I identify as heterosexual but I do think about women sometimes and I think I'd like to explore that—but I have no idea how.

I had sex with my same-sex best friend. She freaked out and I've vowed never to touch a woman again. How do I respond to homophobia?

What do you think of NAMBLA (North American Man/Boy Love Association)?

What is good lesbian sex?

I've been with one woman and one man, but I don't know if I am bi-
*   sexual or lesbian.*

Male homosexuality—genetic? Developmental? Both?

6. DEFINITIONS/EXPLAIN THIS . . .

How does sex feel when you're pregnant?

How do females ejaculate?

How common are sex parties?

Is there good sex after Vassar?

Discuss multiple sex partners.

Anal sex—is it safe? Good? Bad? Anything?

How does a woman ejaculate?

7. MASTURBATION

Does masturbation enjoyment significantly affect sex with others?

How can I help a female friend get over thinking that masturbation
*   is disgusting? She's even sickened by the subject.*

How many ways are there for women to masturbate?

Can you masturbate too much?

Is it a sign of insecurity to masturbate after sex if your partner hasn't
*   satisfied you?*

If I can't masturbate, will I never come, even during sex?

What are some ways I can pleasure myself?

Is it true that if you use a vibrator you will become dependent and
*   unable to have orgasm manually?*

I've tried masturbating and find that I can get turned on but I can't
*   seem to climax. Any tips?*

8. COMMUNICATION

How do you keep sex interesting in a long-term monogamous relationship?

How can sexual tension be maintained in a long-term relationship?

Say I'm really curious about something sexual, like, it sounds awfully cool, and I try it with a partner and it feels WEIRD. Okay. That's embarrassing. How do I suggest trying it differently without hurting my friend's feelings?

Would you tell a new partner if you were uneasy about how to have sex these days (can't let go), or would you keep quiet about it to keep from jinxing the situation?

I project an image of the Great Prude. I am not a prude, if my imagination is any clue. However, shyness always gets in my way. How can I become sexier without going overboard—changing radically?

Why do people always say "are you having sex" and presume it means one thing? Oral sex is not equal to vaginal sex is not equal to anal sex, but damn it, it all counts.

How do you know when a person's serious?

I want to have sex with a man I don't know very well. How can I attract him?

Why can't I approach women—even at Vassar!

I'm in a relationship with someone who is a virgin and wants to stay that way—but I want to make love with them . . . what to do?

At what point does being open about sexuality become harassment of the public?

How do you know if you've pleased someone sexually?

What's a good way to get yourself to open your mouth and tell your partner how to satisfy you—if you're shy, inhibited, etc.

9. TOOLS OF THE TRADE

Can you give some advice about the use of sex toys during mastur-
bation?
What is the safest way to sterilize leather sex toys?
What are some good sex videos?
Dildos—why?
What kind of flavored heating lubricant would you recommend? I
found the one I tried to be a big disappointment.
Where can I find the best vibrators?
If you're having sex with a woman, why use a dildo?
What about vegetable dildos?
Where's the best place to keep the K-Y/Astroglide/etc.?
Do you know if the new "tongue" vibrator is any good?
Can you explain the strap-on dildo thing—how, etc.—I know noth-
ing.
Will they ever market dental dams for sexual use?

10. EROTIC COMPATIBILITY

Can stylistic differences be overcome? If yes, how? For example, S/M
preference vs. gentle and tender lovemaking?
Why aren't I attracted to someone who is like me?
Why does the male perspective of sex differ from the female, i.e.,
locker-room talk?
Why do I seem to meet so many women who bring a political agenda
to sex?
Why does plain vanilla sex become less and less satisfying?
I'm really happy in my relationship in every sense except sexually.
Suggestions?
I'm into light S/M, my partner is not. What can be done about this?
Also, any recommendations for two "tops"?

Why do I want to be sexually involved with people when I am constantly unsatisfied?

Should I fool around with someone I don't like because I need sex?

Do you think it is better to be in love with someone with whom you are having regular sex? Is it bad if they love you, but you don't feel the same?

Is gender more important than the individual? I.e., would someone rather have sex with a jerk of correct gender or with someone cool, no matter what gender?

11. SEDUCTION

How do you get a woman to sleep with you or how do you flirt with women?

How can I get some gay sex here?

Without becoming active in the gay community, how am I supposed to find a girlfriend?

How do you seduce straight (questionably straight) people? How do you sustain flirting, romance, etc. in a long-term relationship?

Why am I only attracted to men I can never make (straight men)?

Why can't I seem to get any? Everyone else does. How do I make myself clearly available without losing my pride or decorum?

Why do I scare men off when I talk about sex openly and freely?

Why do I love the idea of having sex and flirting, but when it gets down to it, I want to get sick?

Why am I so deathly afraid of rejection even though I am hot and bothered twenty-four hours a day?

Do any guys like women for reasons other than physical attractions?

What are successful flirting techniques?

12. COMMUNICATION AND INTUITION

How can I enjoy sex more?

I can't tell when my boyfriend has come. How can I tell?

How do you know when something is supposed to feel good, or be enjoyable; and if it's supposed to be and it's not, what's wrong?

Why are we so inhibited?

What is the best way to discuss with your partner improving your sex life?

What makes some people so intuitively wonderful at sex, while others may be more experienced, yet suck?

13. ABUSE

How can I avoid getting flashbacks during sex? Or what should I do when I have them?

How do you enjoy sex after you've been raped?

After you have been violated by a woman at the age of ten . . . Twelve years later you are crazy about a beautiful woman . . . how do you get over it?

14. TURN-OFFS

Have you ever been afraid of a penis?

How can I avoid the "turn-off" switch when my lover does me?

How can I convince myself to be turned on to other women?

What if I just don't feel like it someday?

What should you do if your boyfriend's fantasies disgust you? . . . And he insists on doing this "You're fourteen years old" shit . . .

15. EROTIC FANTASIES

Can you be a lesbo and still be immensely turned on by erections? (Penile, I mean.)

193

Does fantasizing about lesbian sex make you a lesbian?

Is it normal to think about having sex with more than one person?

What does an increase in wet dreams indicate?

How can you always, or often, want to have sex with so many other more pressing things to do in your life?

I've heard that rape fantasies are common for women. Is this true? Is it okay to explore with a partner?

Why have I dreamt on two separate occasions about two different people I know but am not attracted to—they approached me for sex but I said no. What does it mean?

How do you interpret your fantasies?

I'm really turned on by the idea of impregnating a female partner, although I don't intend to have kids anytime soon. What does this indicate?

Why do I like rape fantasies?

What do I do if I run out of erotic fantasies?

Could you talk about submission?

Why am I turned on by the thought of sex with a gay man?

Does everyone have bisexual fantasies?

Why am I obsessed with giving people hickeys on their necks?

Why do I want to be dominated and abused sexually, basically made powerless?

Why don't I have many fantasies?

What about fantasies about group sex?

Why, as a straight female, do I get turned on by sex with a homosexual male?

Why is it that I desire to sleep with two voluptuous women at once?

Why does only the thought of having sex with gay men turn me on?

Why do I fantasize about threesomes?

Why do I get rid of my own fantasies?

16. BODY IMAGE

How do you get to be comfortable with your body?
Comment on standards of beauty in homosexual culture.
I don't like having sex in the daylight. What can I do to feel better about my body?

17. SEXUAL REPRESENTATION

Why is sex in movies so serious?

18. LOVE AND LUST

Why do I place so much value on the affection attached to sex?
Do lesbians really like sex? I come across so many women who just want to be friends. Is it all love and no sex for lesbians?
How can a person have a one-night stand and still talk to the person they hooked up with?
Can sex ever be unemotional? Are there always strings attached?
How can I explore sexually without making sex cheap?
Why don't people respect that I plan to marry my first sexual partner?
Does lack of enjoyment mean lack of love?
Why can't others understand that sleeping with an experienced 46-year-old has been really special, beautiful, and satisfying?

19. MORALITY AND ETHICS

Is it wrong to have many lovers?
What about sex shouldn't be public? Should anything be kept secret or cryptic?
Is there something wrong with consistently having relations with a person who is considerably older than you? Or with someone who is in a position of power over you?

195

Why do we have the young vs. older hang-up?
How can you be bisexual and monogamous?

20. DISEASE

*Can you catch oral herpes from someone if they aren't breaking out
   at the time you kiss them?*
What is a dental dam? Are they necessary for safe oral sex?
I want a compelling reason to use protection with women.
*I'm worried about getting STDs from giving blowjobs. So I generally
   don't give them. The problem is that now I'd really like to give a
   guy the pleasure—what can I do?*

I realize that many of my readers may be reading these questions,
especially the "name-that-tune" technique questions, and wondering if they already have the correct answers at their fingertips.
There are a few books I recommend, the "classics" that answer
virtually all the questions these students wrote down on their index cards. For questions of technique, physiology, toys, all that
how-does-it-work stuff, the best of the best are:

The Good Vibrations Book of Sex by Cathy Winkes and Anne
   Semans

The Erotic Mind by Jack Morin

The New Male Sexuality by Bernie Zilbergeld

Sex for One by Betty Dodson, plus her video *SelfLoving*

The Playbook for Kids About Sex by Joani Blank

196

Totally Offensive

Totally Offensive

What we showed was that there was an evil being transmitted directly into the house, with no controls, with no way of stopping it," said Donna Rice-Hughes of "Enough Is Enough." We wanted to know what they were going to do about it.

—"HOW BARE-KNUCKLED POLITICS WON DECENCY FIGHT,"
BY HOWARD BRYANT AND DAVID PLOTNIKOFF,
SAN JOSE MERCURY NEWS

LAST SUMMER A LITTLE dream of mine came true. I was invited to teach a course of my choice at the University of California at Santa Cruz, and I suggested the subject "The Politics of Sexual Representation," or as I nicknamed it, "Porn 101." My official title might have sounded pretentious, but it was quite specific about what I wanted to accomplish with my students: an understanding of what our society considers to be a sexual image, and whether that picture of sex is considered healthy and moral or destructive and alien, masculine or feminine, black or white—our society's take on the erotic body. Commercial pornography would serve as one of our primary "texts," since this is what most people consider unfiltered and explicit sexual imagery.

Over the course of the summer, we had plenty of sexual politics in the news to talk about, and we'd usually spend the first minutes in class going over the latest in prurient current events. No subject held the American media audience more in thrall that summer than the specter of the Internet, the erotic possibilities of online technology— where, according to those in the know, you could see and hear everything under the sun, in a little electronic world immune to censorship, accountable to nobody except the interest of its participants.

The come-ons we heard about surfing the Web took on freak show proportions. Was sex on the Internet the wildest show yet? What could be SO taboo that only the most gee-whiz technology was able to let it out of the bag? I asked my students what they thought might be the most outrageous dirty pictures to be found on the Net. They had quick answers for me: Animals. Extreme S/M. Snuff films. Interestingly, they didn't immediately think of "kiddie porn," but maybe it's because most of them still get called "kid" and are intuitively sick of the condescension. When I asked THEM where they had gotten their first glimpses of "dirty pictures," none of them said the Internet—it was strictly from *Playboy* and other well-inked periodicals, typically found in and around their parents' home, and thoroughly scrutinized between the ages of five and nine.

One day, my most techno-savvy student brought in a copy of *Time* magazine, whose cover had a wide-angle picture of a blue-eyed blond-haired boy gaping in shock at the fried glare of a computer screen. I laughed, and asked if it was a cover story on the scandalous details of Bill Gates's childhood, because that was who the stunned little junior resembled.

But Steve, my student, corrected me in a hurry. This cover story was an exposé about how porn was filling up 80 percent of the Internet's airwaves, and how any moron or juvenile with a home or school computer could be viewing this depravity. My stomach turned. What a strange sensation to feel the beginning of a lie, a little piece of propaganda that promised a full-scale panic, and not be able to do a damn thing about it. If it were possible to pick up the telephone that very minute to reach *Time*'s editor, all I could have whispered was, "How could you?"

I started reading the *Time* story out loud to my students to see what all the fuss was about, and as I did, my indignation turned to amazement. The key research that provided *Time*'s reporters with their story of the online porno menace was a study project by a man named Martin Rimm, an undergraduate research student at Carnegie-Mellon University.

Marty Rimm! I knew Marty Rimm, and he had been e-mailing me for the past several months, portraying himself as a porn-sympathetic, fearless researcher who held MY work on women's erotica and antiporn analysis in the highest regard. He acted like he was the last word in porno expertise, and he seemed to measure his ego by the number of X-rated images he'd downloaded.

I was introduced to Rimm, by the way, because of a free-speech attorney named Mike Godwin, who encouraged me to start an e-mail correspondence with some very sharp women students at Carnegie-Mellon who called themselves, with appropriate panache, The Clitoral Hoods.

The Hoods were up in arms because their school administration—and this is a school known for their state-of-the-art science and engineering programs—decided to stop their students from accessing "sex" on their Internet connections, so as not to corrupt or defile their youthful sensibilities. The Hoods, as well as a lot of other students and faculty, did not appreciate their administration's paternalism and were organizing to overturn the new censorship rules.

Marty Rimm first contacted me through his "friends" in the Hoods; he introduced himself by telling me that he was publishing a study about online porn in the prestigious Georgetown *Law Journal*, and that I could ask "five questions" about it. Who said I wanted to? I thought that was a very peculiar way to introduce oneself. He also sought some citations from my essays on porn.

Everything about the way Marty communicated was odd. He

told me he was working on a series of inspirational articles about me, Camille Paglia, and Catherine MacKinnon, which seemed like a weird trio of heroines. How could he love me and Kitty at the same time? Our only connection is that we have both watched a lot more pornography than most women—and that probably summed up his interest too. Marty seemed like a classic porn-dog raincoater—the kind of guy who can't communicate very well to real women but dreams of being surrounded by porn stars. Me, Kitty, and Camille were probably just his idea of intellectual smut queens.

I informed my students at our next class, all of us a little stunned, that this *Time* cover story was not only a nasty little farce, it was also something for which I had personally been flimflammed. This Rimm character could not possibly be an earnest antiporn advocate on the Net—he'd apparently been playing both sides to feed his own enormous ego. Furthermore, his deceit had paid off, for the *Time* article was now being waved about on the Congress floor as prima-facie evidence for the evil consequences of uncensored telecommunications. Marty was instantly famous: the new darling of vice-squad law enforcement, the religious right wing, and his special crush, Catherine MacKinnon. I figured he must be pretty happy except for the fact that he had just burned his bridges as far as meeting any porn stars was concerned.

I remembered how confusing Marty's mail had been sometimes. One of the Hoods told me that, as far as anyone could tell, Marty was way into porn, but that he would get grossed out by things that he thought went too far. He would draw a line at anything that was too kinky for his tastes, although his taste seemed to change based on who he was talking to. He didn't think that women could appreciate or be turned on to most graphic sexual images, and he was uncomfortable defending free speech considerations. My Clitoral Hood correspondents had taken pity on him; they were convinced that if he were exposed to more outspoken feminist pornographers and porn-appreciative women, he would grow some guts. They must certainly be ready to eviscerate him now.

Well, Rimm is not alone in his ambivalence and gutlessness. I hear from men like Marty all the time, who have one foot in the closet of shame, but one toe sticking out—just in case the coast is clear. This sort of man will write to me, essentially asking for a blessing on his own erotic fantasies, while putting down other people's turn-ons which he judges deviant. It's always a step in the right direction when a closet case confesses, but when these declarations are made at the expense of someone else's erotic integrity, they have to be nipped in the bud. I can't hand them the flower of sexual liberation if they think it's just going to be me and them alone, at last, with our disdain to keep us company.

Still, of all the fans and curiosity seekers who've approached me through the mail, none had ever turned into the KINGPIN of cyber-porn research! Not only that, but Martin Rimm had hoodwinked everyone. He'd flattered and sucked up to anybody who might publicize or help further his efforts, but he never seemed to get the point that the jig was up. As fast as he made his celebrity bed with the censorship brigade, his little report was being ripped to pieces by Internet activists, civil liberties attorneys, and anyone with a modicum of common sense—after all, if 80 percent of the Web is pornographic, we'd hardly need Marty to "expose" anything.

A few weeks after the *Time* magazine article appeared and his reputation was in tatters on the Net, Rimm e-mailed me again for a small favor: "Dear Susie, If you don't hate me now like everyone else, would you please . . ."

Oh, no, Marty-kins, how could I hate you? You just instigated the most disgusting censorship campaign since the McCarthy trials! Our government was threatening to turn the online world into some version of Romper Room, and he wanted sympathy.

Marty often either talked like a little boy begging for Mommy's approval, or, when he turned to his macho persona, he resembled The Riddler in a *Batman* episode. In his superhero conceit, he would present information like it was a three-card monte game in the back of a train. I always asked him to be blunt with me, to tell me what he was after, what he really believed, but it was like an amusement park ride—I just kept getting sick to my stomach.

I suppose many other assholes could have spurred a porno scare on the Internet; if it hadn't been Marty, it would have been some other opportunist's dirty little job. But his two-faced brazenness made him an extreme version of the typical law-enforcement porn-dog personality. These kinds of men are OBSESSED with pornography; they know every porn star's name, every position, every cum shot—yet their professional lives are dedicated to stamping it out. Of course, if porn was truly stamped out, they'd be out of a job and deprived of their obsession—and then would they ever be unhappy!

I think if Marty was given the same kind of opportunities as John Wayne Bobbitt and was afforded the chance to wave his dick in front of a camera and newly siliconed starlets, he'd jump at it. Or maybe he'd like to direct. Rimm did offer a glimpse of his porno entrepreneur talents when he authored a companion piece to his official Georgetown study—yes, Marty did two versions of the same clown act. The version NOT promoted by *Time,* called *The Pornographer's Handbook: How to Exploit Women, Dupe Men, and Make Lots of Money,* is a get-rich-quick manual for online porn purveyors, and it answers such questions as "How many facial cum shots should I have on my adult BBS?"

Marty took all his prized knowledge about what porn on the Net is most popular and turned it into a smut-peddler's dream marketing scheme. Throw the dice, Marty! Rimm bragged to me about writing this very book and told me it was in the mail to me for my perusal and praise; but, gosh, it just never arrived. Luckily, somebody leaked some of his chapters from this gospel onto the USENET, and they reveal not only his bullshit for every occasion but also his special sexual point of view.

"The slightest indication of pain can make some men limp," Marty explains in how to broadcast the "best anal sex image." "Indeed," he goes on, "his orgasm is often contingent upon seeing the woman feel no pain, because if she feels no pain it means that she will willingly engage in such acts on a regular basis."

It's HIS orgasm all right; Marty is apparently talking about himself here, his own limpness, his incomprehension that women might actually like anal sex for their own reasons. His interpretations don't have a single empirical—or researched—leg to stand on.

Marty's guilt goes overboard again when he warns, in his "KINK" section, "Remember that people log onto your board because they do not have full control over their libidos." Oooh, you're scary, Marty, that's the conservative rapist's point of view, too! Get this guy away from us!

When Rimm started getting investigated for all his dubious manipulations, he said that this manual was a satire, but I don't think so—it reads an awful lot like the piece he wrote for Georgetown. And I don't think he is satirizing his own Jurassic attitudes about sexuality. As is usual for prudish porn-dogs, Marty is not really describing anything but himself and his own sexual hang-ups.

What was so infuriating and frightening about the *Time* article was the political influence it had on already opportunistic lawmakers who were already more than happy to shut down democratic access to EVERYTHING, using the demonization of porn as their Trojan horse. God damn it, dirty pictures never killed anybody, and sexual speech is as human as it gets, but when faced with elitism and the sword of puritanical righteousness, free speech and democratic access seem to enjoy only the slenderest of chances.

If anything good came out of the *Time* report, it was the enthusiasm the students in my little class were given to investigate the Net themselves. My student Steve, who'd originally brought the magazine to class, decided to go into the dirty-picture places from which Marty had presumably taken his samples (although, to be fair, Marty almost exclusively used private bulletin boards for his porn research). From there, Steve downloaded examples which, by the written description, matched Marty's categories of pornography. Then the whole class looked at each picture, which is probably more than Marty ever did—he probably just looked at his favorites and grouped the others by description alone.

Well, what kind of pictures did we see in our classroom? Everyone was terribly disappointed after all the buildup. In the bestiality section, there were the typical Internet animal jokes: you'd see a file called "Pussy Sex" and then you'd open it up and there'd be two lions doing it in the shade. Ha, ha. There was a picture of a dog with an erection—"Ewww," several people said—and then a picture of someone's hand stroking it. We had a long talk about when we first saw, as children, an animal doing it with another animal, and what we thought it was all about.

Next up were the pictures that implied that a child was involved. These pictures all seemed to be scanned copies of things that appeared in some seventies porn magazine. There was a picture of a woman—obviously over thirty—wearing saddle shoes with a dreadful wig that sported pigtails. We've all seen better Lolita kitsch in *Playboy*. Then there were pictures of naked young men who could have been anywhere from sixteen to twenty-five—nice smooth bodies, a snapshot of one diving into a pond, another picture of a group hanging out in a meadow. This didn't evoke any particular sense of the forbidden, as all these men were past puberty. Finally we looked at some S/M pictures, including ones that featured permanent piercings and "play" piercings (where you use feather-slight needles to make a design, then remove them). Like every group of people under thirty today, my class had their own full biographies of various piercings and tattoos, so these pictures only seemed to provoke the usual beauty parlor–style gossip that accompanies every vanity application.

In the end, although every picture Steve downloaded was a conversation piece, the overall response of the class was, "Is that it?"

"Of course that's not all," I said. "I'm sure we could find SOMETHING out there on the Internet, if we had the time, that would shock the pants off of you. But the point is, you don't have to go to the Internet to stumble across images that upset you; they are readily available in the print media—and what's more, they're already in your own mind. All of us have a sense of what goes too far— a line drawn—and we can only draw that line if we have an imaginative glimpse of what the forbidden is."

The Offensive Game

ONE DAY IN CLASS, I told everyone to push the chairs out of the way and get ready to draw. I had about a hundred colored pens in my purse and a huge roll of butcher paper. I told them to get comfy with pen in hand, because I was going to ask them to draw a few images for me.

First off, I wanted them to draw something nonerotic, nonsexual, that truly offended them. It had to gross them out and upset them in the worst way. I told them it should be very personal, and that I didn't care if it was the most common thing in the world or the weirdest—be true to your offended senses!

I gave them a couple of examples that upset me. I can't watch those commercials about people who have bloodshot eyes and use medicated eye drops to relieve themselves. As soon as the camera gets close to their red-veined eyeballs and the liquid-filled dropper ready to burst, I'm outta that room! I can't take it! It nauseates me. Here's another thing I hate: I can't read stories about parents who torture their children—the whole feces-smeared, locked-in-a-closet scenario—I can hardly bear to describe it. It doesn't even have to be presented to me as a picture, for I find it visceral enough to hear those stories on the radio, or read them in print. It makes me feel hysterical, both violated and violent.

I chose these two examples because I realized one sounds silly and oversensitive (the eyedrops commercial) while the other is universally condemned and vilified. I wanted my students to see that both these things "get to me," even though they have totally different social contexts. The point of our exercise was to examine our sensual reactions, not be concerned about what others would think of them.

After they finished their masterpiece, I asked them to start a second drawing. This one would be something extremely offensive to them that was sexual. The definition of "sexual" was up to them; I wasn't going to narrow the boundaries. Just to get the ball rolling, I told them that despite everyone's laughter the other day at the bogus Internet animal-porn pictures, I myself found the sight of raw, red dog erections completely loathsome, and that was one of the reasons I was a diehard cat lover. I quickly drew a yucky dog with his yucky dick on the blackboard. My other example, I said, was the sexual fetish for scat, for shit—anything sexual that had to do with feces made me sick. Before I had a baby, I used to wonder how on earth I was ever going to get used to dirty diapers, and I certainly couldn't imagine tending to adults in the same situation, like any nurse would do. I don't like shit, period, and the idea that it could be paired with eroticism is anathema to me.

I emphasized that the sexual offensiveness picture only had to reflect our personal "unbearable" feelings, not our beliefs about whether such an image or behavior should be banned.

We finished our pictures and hung them on the wall. My head swam looking at the images, because without any words next to them, they looked so similar that I couldn't tell which was sex and which was not. Blood, cum, peanut butter, snot—it was all sticky. We took turns guessing what the pictures were, and all hope of anonymity fell apart as each student was moved to claim their own grotesque vision. Our gallery of horrors was described like this:

1. "A woman deep-throating a man with a huge cock"
2. "A gang rape where the men are stabbing my woman friend"
3. "Macaroni and cheese—the taste, smell, the leftovers, the dirty dishes"
4. "Government-sanctioned violence" (a drawing of a man in a noose, with official-looking men looking on and applauding)
5. "Peanut products, especially peanut butter"
6. "Bare feet, especially when people try to pick things up between their toes"
7. "IV drug tracks on someone's skin"
8. "A dripping snatch, a wet smelly pussy"
9. "The gimp from *Pulp Fiction,* and my ex-boyfriend who works at 7-11"
10. "A parent verbally abusing a child who has already been beaten"
11. "Ball gags, hoods—any kind of suffocation device, also cuttings and blood"
12. "Religious hypocrites" (a drawing of a church leader giving an antigay sermon while being sucked off by a youth under the pulpit)
13. "A young woman who is pregnant and is still a child herself"
14. "Deforestation of the Central American rain forest to promote violence against animals and American meat consumption"
15. "Drawing blood" (a drawing of a hypodermic filling up from an arm)
16. "Lies, any kind of lies" (a drawing of hot black bubbles coming from heads)
17. "A group of people emotionally dictating the death penalty, especially for all to observe"
18. "Neglected animals" (a drawing of a starving dog tied up to a post)
19. "Swallowing men's cum"
20. "A fat chick getting head"

21. "Scat, eating 'shit-sickles' " (a drawing of popsicles made out of poop)
22. "A big ass covered with hair and zits"

The overlap between erotic and noneorotic fell into place as I listened to the descriptions of what they'd drawn. First, we had the image of excess: a fat chick, a big ass, a giant jar of peanut butter, a huge cock, a gang bang, a giant dirty toe. The body is huge in fantasy; it's like those balloons drifting overhead at Macy's parade. Not only is the body enormous, but it has a powerful odor too. Hardly a single picture didn't entail bodily fluids or things reminiscent of bodily fluids, all with a powerful smell or taste. We had semen, blood, peanut butter, macaroni, shit-sickles, and the hilarious dripping pussy juice so expertly drawn by the youngest gay man in class.

Enormous sizes and pungent smells led our hit parade—and then, most horrifically and cathartically, we could see our pictured bodies violated, a hole in the body. In our collection, we saw rape and needles, objects going in and coming out of anus, cunt, mouth. Sometimes the aftereffect of penetration was the poignant image: pregnancy, scars, tracks. There was the image of the body whole and intact, and then an opening into the body; that broken boundary epitomized a sense of loss and helplessness.

Helplessness was the outraged voice of our offensive pictures: the appearance of the weak/innocent (children, animals, vulnerable women) being preyed on by the strong/powerful (powerful men and/ or adults). The big people, as I called them, with their big hypocrisy and gross corruption, were sketched specifically as politicians, church leaders, and parents manipulating children, in addition to the anonymous threatening male figure. I dared to laugh at the "deforestation of the rain forest" picture, only to find myself booed and reprimanded by the entire class. They identified with the preyed-upon wildlife as much as they did with the human victims in their pictures.

We all laughed a lot actually; there was hardly anything else to do when confronted with all our psychic entrails. The red and black pens were all worn out. It seemed easy to recognize how ugly the abuse of power can be, but the penetrated body and its leavings were even more bedeviling. All of us, at some moments, welcome the point of entry, the opening of our skins and ourselves to another body, giving it up. The risk is titillating; it has the capacity to be so wonderful and maybe so awful.

At our next class, I decided to look at the differences between those pictures we'd drawn, the pictures of violence and sexuality in our mind, and the real-life violence we'd experienced. I asked everyone to quickly write down the most violent thing that ever happened to them personally, and this is what they told me:

"A drunk, violent, drag-out fight between me and Greg. Wanting to kill each other. Scared how much I wanted to cause harm. I broke my wrist and fractured two ribs. He was a bloody pulp. It really got scary when we both had our knives out about to stab each other. I never thought either of us could be so violent."

"My mother was angry at me and my sister for not cleaning up our room. She had us lay on her bed facedown, pants off. She pulled our hands behind our backs and spanked us. I remember trying so hard to free my hands."

"I was in eighth grade, the worst year of my life. One morning I went to put my books in my locker. As soon as I turned around, I was hit hard by another kid who was a long-time enemy. I was shocked and didn't react in time. I got the shit kicked out of me—yet the worst part was the crying—I also got into more fights because of it."

"Getting mugged."

"Getting an abortion."

"My father kicked my ass."

None of my students had lived through a war-time situation or any of the violent escapades they see in their dreams or on TV. The brutality in their lives centered around family episodes, lovers, schoolmates, and the occasional street altercation.

Next, I asked them what was the worst violence they ever witnessed, but which didn't directly touch their body:

"I was with my grade-school class at Cocoa Beach when the *Challenger* shuttle exploded in the air. Everyone kept asking, 'What happened? What happened?' and then the teacher took us out of there real fast."

"Last week my house mate slit his wrists and blood was all over the bathroom and dripped on the sofa. Today he's home and recovering, but the staples in his cuts are such a scary reminder of that night."

"I was at a demonstration that got out of control, the police were beating people with their clubs, it was such a sickening sound."

"Seeing a goat get de-butted."

"It was on the bus. This gay kid always sat in front. I've never seen anyone more verbally abused by their peers. 'Fag' and 'fudge packer' were favorite names to call him. Sometimes they would try to make him sit on the floor."

"Watching a man run down the street to beat another man with a two-by-four."

"My parents fought so bad I left home."

This time the list of violence included more strangers, and also the anticipation of something awful happening, or the aftermath, without seeing the act itself. Yet like witnesses, the students filled in the visuals for themselves. The threat of violence was close enough to create a vicarious experience.

Finally, I asked them to note the worst violence they'd ever seen pictures of or read about, something that haunted them that was never even close to them in reality:

"Pictures and documentaries of the extermination camps during World War II."

"Reading the book *American Psycho* by Bret Easton Ellis."

"Jodie Foster's rape scene in *The Accused* was pretty bad."

"The San Ysidro McDonald's restaurant massacre."

"Those old war images, people being blown apart."

"The movie *Sibyl* really got to me. We watched it in psychology class in high school and I was so upset I had to put my head down. The fact that it was a true story about child abuse really made me sick. I couldn't deal with the pain inflicted upon this poor little girl."

"The scene in the film *Reservoir Dogs* where the guy's ear is cut off."

Sharing these memories was one of the few times the whole class could moan and agree with each other; they are all about the same age and have seen these movies, been to McDonald's, been presented with the literature and documentary of war. It was interesting to me that their most horrific war pictures came to them from World War II, whereas for me, Vietnam comes quickly and overwhelmingly to mind. Some of the images that upset them are the sort of thing restricted to minors, like the R-rated films they mentioned, but the horror of real-life news and the banality of a high-school message movie were just as competitive for their anxious attention.

My classroom's experience with terror and bodily risk was, more than anything, dictated by their class background, as the students were largely middle- and upper-middle-class Americans living in a country where the only terrorism is homegrown and largely familial. Their ability to be shocked by nasty things like bestiality, for example, has a lot more to do with whether they grew up on a farm than whether their father had a secret collection of porn videos. What has really shocked them is vicious battles with people they loved, the survival of the fittest in the schoolroom—the alienation of neighbor from neighbor, citizen from citizen—and, most arbitrarily, the calamitous acts of God—the senseless, thoughtless accidents. Is the last an evil that enters our homes and blinds us with its thrill and sensation? Or is it fury itself, the brutal fate that knocks people right out of this world without a thought for good intentions?

We make love and we make war, and the best and the worst of us get ravaged. I must get offended, everyone must get offended: if you didn't know how to draw a line, you wouldn't have anything to defend, would you? Being offended is natural, and our list of offenses is our modern oracle. What's not natural is thinking that putting a lid on it, pulling the plug, whitewashing the news, trying to get that damn spot out, is going to make anything better, anything safer— that it's going to save our souls or plug our holes. Legislating our morality, legislating against sexual representation has all the righteousness of banning big toes and peanut butter, except it will do a lot more damage to our lives. Sex itself is no evil handmaiden to brutality, but it is a sign of life bursting through the opening, the rare opening, that is just entirely big enough.

Cruising

I DON'T KNOW IF Apple, Inc., ever learned this—they certainly wouldn't congratulate me or anyone else for it—but the first, the very first magazine that was entirely laid out on computer, with what was just barely desktop publishing software on a Macintosh, was a lesbian sex magazine called *On Our Backs*. Back then the magazines that covered computers would never have dreamed of using computer production methods because they were so . . . primitive. My partners and I had a magazine with incredible content, startling photography, and taboo-breaking text, but it was all set in the clunkiest, ugliest design you ever saw in your life.

I actually cried when my partner Debi at *On Our Backs* told me we had to figure out how to make our mag on computer—or go bust from paying the typesetter bills. I told her I didn't see how I could do it. After all, I could barely type, I thought an IBM Selectric was frightening. I loved writing longhand on a fat stack of yellow legal pads. How on earth did she expect me to run a computer?

Debi, meanwhile, made so much money in tips as a stripper that she could afford to march right out and buy a state-of-the-art Macintosh, and she had an entrepreneurial boy's spirit for appreciating new toys. She told me my machine anxieties were irrelevant. She put

216

me in front of her computer screen and told me to listen to a little instructional tape that they used to include with your purchase when you bought the first PCs. The tape had somebody who sounded like Captain Kangaroo telling me to push the big button on the top. That was easy. I kind of felt it might all be that simple, like one of those psychological tests where you get to pick colored blocks and fit them into holes.

Then the tape told me to move this hand object, called a mouse, around on a little pad. When I moved the mouse, a little graphic arrow on the screen also moved around; it was similar to those old Etch-A-Sketch pads I was given as a child, where you were supposed to turn the knobs and draw a dinosaur. I started to panic again. I could barely render a plain box on the Etch-A-Sketch, as I recalled. But Captain Kangaroo kept talking in a soothing voice and, a few minutes later, I was moving mousie around like it was catnip. This was easy. It had nothing to do with math, with testosterone, with being an athletic success or drawing straight lines without flinching. I looked at my screen and saw a girl's best friend.

I'm not exaggerating about what a terrible sissy I am, and this before-and-after story rivals anybody's one-hundred-pound weight-loss testimonial. The computer is wonderful for me; it is filled with the evidence of my relationships with other people, and yet when I read the news about computers, or the computer trade magazines, nobody ever seems to talk about the people angle—which for me is the only angle worth talking about.

Now there is a notable exception to the computer press coverage. When they're not talking about bytes and stock shares and modem speeds and CD-ROM capacity, there is one people-oriented aspect of computers that everyone, just everyone does hear about: HORNY PERVERTS contacting you over the airwaves and RUINING your life. SEDUCING your children. SAPPING you of your moral strength and stamina. FILTHY PICTURES, supplied by even filthier people, who just can't seem to do anything but suck on the giant computer tit of uncensored SMUT. Yes, that's it, it's computers as smut tits.

As scandalous as the reports are, downloading sex is the one time when anyone actually admits that the computer functions as if it were a person who could reach out and touch you—that it is a people facilitator, not just a bunch of fascinating ones and zeros for the pocket-protector set. Of course, this personal quality is demonized in the perversion reportage: it's hysterical, it's today's version of reefer madness and hippie cannibal fantasies. And in the same way as hearing how drugs and rock and roll will turn you on, the sex madness of the computer scare is very intoxicating. Even people who wouldn't look at a *Playboy* centerfold if it was handed to them on the toilet are aroused into action by their curiosity. What is it that is so HORRIBLE, so beyond the pale, that it can only be accessed by freewheeling computer owners? Let's buy a modem and find out!

I think when the computer manufacturers send you that little card with your product that asks you how old you are, where you bought the machine, etcetera, they should also ask, "How long did it take you to go look for the pornography on line?" Five minutes? Two weeks, tops? Even if you're scared, it's obvious that you can hide behind your keyboard. No one can see or hear you, no one can show up at your doorstep if you don't give them the address. In this way it's perfect for sissies and girls who know the usual penalties for sexual adventure.

If I walked out on the street and asked a group of men who had the biggest dick, and would he please pull it out—well, fill in the blanks yourself. It's never going to happen on my real street, but it's easy as pie to do it on Virtual Street. You can be the biggest juvenile giggler, the most audacious ball-buster, the most genuinely innocent and curious, and it is almost impossible not to get a response. And if you don't like it, you can do one better than "hang up"—you can make the screen go completely black. It has a vanquishing effect.

I didn't get a modem for the longest time. I was still hung up about its possible complications; I was caught in the old phobia that it was technologically beyond me. No one ever said, look, it's like installing a phone line in your computer—period. Then you go places by dialing numbers, and there are groups of people sitting around and you can talk with them, like a party line, or go off and speak to someone alone.

I used to do this exact sort of thing on the phone in junior high school. There was a rumor among my friends that if you dialed certain numbers you would get an open party line: first you'd hear nothing, then someone would say, "Any chicks out there?" and then you'd hear them breathing, and somebody else would just mumble "Big tits," and then some brave little snot would announce she was having a party and wanted only "cute guys" to come over, but you'd stay on the line for an hour and she'd never actually say where she lived.

This little demi-monde is EXACTLY what you will find if you go into a typical "chat room" of one of the many bulletin board services that are so popular today. It's kind of a drag when you're looking to find big hairy pornography and all you can find is somebody in an America Online chat room mumbling "Big tits."

If you're like me, you say to yourself, how can anyone utter the words "big tits" or cruise for sex in a place like America Online when the company is always bragging how they have untold numbers of police monitors, scouring the lines for people who use bad words, and promptly eighty-sixing them from the service? You even hear about how their own prudishness makes fools out of the service administration, like when they banned the word "breast" and then started throwing out members of the entirely serious breast cancer survivors support group that met regularly online.

I got in a big fight myself when I gave an interview to AOL. A few minutes after I used the word "penis" in answering a question, I was barred from saying "clitoris"! Clit is on their list of banned words, I guess, along with all the words for other parts of the female body. Ironically, if you left my public discussion area and went to see what people were saying in the chat rooms adjacent to my interview, you would find some joker demanding to know, "Who wants to suck my big one?" I didn't dare ask just how big his clit really was.

AOL actually does have a bunch of zealous monitors, but the real chance of being caught by one of these cyber-narcs is akin to the chance you have of being caught speeding on a really lonely stretch of Wyoming highway—only even slimmer, because cyberspace is infinitely bigger than an asphalt road.

The uncovering of frightening pornography was clearly not going to happen during a cursory visit to a large corporate online service like AOL. Educated sexual discussion is taboo. I found my interest in online relationships not in the chat rooms, but in the newsrooms. At the height of the O. J. Simpson trial, I discovered the most provocative discussion on AOL: the "O.J. folder." There must have been a million personal reactions in that little folder, and it was better than a Gallup poll. There were a lot of white participants saying things that made me think they lived in a goldfish bowl; then I thought, no, it's just that American life is SEGREGATED for so many people—this is the real thing, not an aberration. There were fewer but some very vocal and self-identified Black voices speaking up, and in contrast to the polls you read, there was not a clear color line about the innocent/guilty issue. Race was also separated from the issue of "whether or not you can BELIEVE the verdict."

I felt myself getting mad that nobody was saying what I believed. But then I had to kick myself, because that's my job, eh? Nobody else was being represented until they spoke up, either. Chat rooms encourage a more uncensored, even impolite discussion of differences than you would find in an in-person discussion. You wouldn't dare go that far in person because you'd worry that somebody would get physical, or that your point would just be lost because you were so damn rude—or that everyone would be talking at once, and you wouldn't get a chance to clarify yourself later. But cyberspace lets you do that; you get to be rude, change your mind, have your turn, and no one punches you in the nose. You can be a little more daring, more indiscreet; and yet the format of writing and seeing responses in turn is a more temperate atmosphere, cultivating democratic discussion in a way that loud voices and big muscles can put a damper on.

When I read posts that I thought were "right on," I would form a little attachment to those posters: I would memorize the writers' handles (their user IDs), and look for more comments by them to see if they said other things I agreed with. I then joined a much smaller online community called the WELL and my infatuations doubled; I was developing crushes on certain people who always seemed to be saying smart, funny, sensitive things to me. I would wonder what they looked like. It was VERY romantic, because I was genuinely falling in love with their minds—it wasn't just superficial, it wasn't big tits, it felt like I was getting to know people the way we OUGHT to, not through superficial glances at their face and figure but from how they shared their thoughts.

Well, this is bullshit, all bullshit—except how romantic these kinds of infatuations feel, because they ARE extremely seductive. I HAVE made good friends online who I never would have met face-to-face, either because they live at the other end of the world or because, if we'd seen each other on the street, we might have taken one glance and thought we had nothing to offer each other.

Still, the idealism of thinking that online relationships are more "honest" leads to plenty of disappointments. People can be very calculating online; it's almost impossible not to be. You sit there and write your little sentences, editing them, getting into your alter ego, knowing that no one can see that your appearance or surroundings belie the impression you're giving in your posts.

Part of the romance is falling in love with the persona you create on line for yourself. When I post on the WELL on any subject, I imagine myself with a cutting wit and brilliant intellect, really sexy and sassy. Sometimes I play dumb to get people to come out of their shell a bit more. Or I tell a story, and it's really a conglomeration of stories edited to make my point. Who's ever going to know the difference? I'm not going to any great lengths to disguise myself—as some people have done on line, changing their gender, race, or entire background; nevertheless, my on-screen image is definitely not quite the same individual you would meet in person. I think it's more flattering. You might think I'm kidding myself. But instead of fooling people with our clothes, our words make the little first impressions, the little white lies. It's a different kind of cover.

The most magnificent dramas happen on line when someone turns out to be RADICALLY different from the way he presented himself. This can be treacherous or poignant or both. To give you an idea of one unforgettable transformation, there was a man I met on the WELL—and only on the WELLl, never face-to-face—named Tom Mandel. His opinions and arguments appeared in every topic and discussion area I traveled to. I knew he was interested in all sorts of politics, but then I'd be poking around in some food discussion, and there he'd be. He worked in the computer press world; he'd obviously been around for years, and I'm sure he had an impressive résumé. Yet I knew him as a very cantankerous, never-at-a-loss-for-words guy who seemed never to leave his computer. He wasn't always right in his opinions, of course—in fact, he upset many people who bozo-filtered him off their screens, or started private conferences where virtually everyone in the world was invited except Tom. I found his crusades and arguments pretty addictive, even when they outraged me. He could dish it out and take it until there were no dishes left in the cupboard.

One day I was in the health conference, which is sort of like a smarty hypochondriacs' conference—it's the ultimate place to complain about your sciatica (I could write a chapter on my sciatica!) and to hear what everyone else is doing about theirs. Medicines, treatments, hospital horror stories, weird things that go bump in the night—it's a great stew of doctors and patients going at it. There's one ongoing topic called "The Bug Report," where you check in to find out the latest flu you're suffering from—that's where I found Tom one day, talking about his awful chest cold that wouldn't go away.

Familiar WELL members, also choked with green mucus and swollen glands, chimed in with all their various strategies and wishes for a fast recovery. We listened to him talk about his latest visits to the doctor, and then one day—just when I was about to send him a big bottle of Nyquil and a garlic wreath—he reported that his doctor had some surprising news. He didn't have a cold after all. He had cancer. Not only did he have cancer, but it was the kind of cancer where you only have days left to say good-bye.

If there was ever a silence on the WELL, this was it. Everything was quiet. When Tom died, people posted "empty" messages, just their user names with blank lines below. That was exactly the way it felt. How could the hugest man, the man who could not and would not shut up, be gone? I cried at his news, and his last words with on-line friends. Alone as I was in my room in front of my screen, I could feel others crying with me. It was that palpable—it wasn't a hallucination or a trance—it was the effect that Tom had had on all of us. People who'd hated his guts were stunned and weeping.

Now here was someone who didn't lie, per se, about who he was; but he was definitely larger than life, impossible to imagine without a voice, or weak, or helpless, or even being cared for. I never thought of Tom as being cared for, or loved, or surrendering like this.

Tom Mandel was perhaps at his most alive—and kicking hard— when the most fantastic deception of all was exposed in my online world. It all started one day in WOW (Women on the WELL), a women's private discussion area. No men are allowed in this area, and none have ever been detected. Every sort of subject is discussed, silly to serious, professional to personal; it feels very much like a group of friends networking and occasionally letting off steam, sharing encouragement and accomplishments, and so forth.

One day I noticed that a couple of women, Gloria and Em, who were well-known posters, had started a topic together called "That Greasy Bastard." With a tag line like that, of course I had to click on it and see who the s.o.b. was. I've changed their names here, and refrained from quoting their words in the private conference—for as you will see, these women's story became a test of how anyone's privacy can be stretched to the limits.

The two women had quite a story to tell. Months earlier, they had both independently received private e-mail from a charming man who they recognized from public conversations on the WELL. He seemed to key into special things that they'd revealed about themselves on line. He wasn't sleazy—quite the opposite. He was boyish, feminist, positive, respectful, funny, and sexy. He developed a real rapport with each woman; they were both fascinated by him, and when the opportunity came up to become erotic with him, it was as easy as falling off their ergonomic chairs. They began to correspond with him regularly, and then graduated to long phone dates.

Imagine piles of steamy e-mail, graduating to even better phone sex—orgasms galore, excitement, intimacy, the feeling that they couldn't leave the phone or the modem alone. Both these women are grown-ups, they've been around the block, and they were not particularly seeking a committed relationship with an unseen man. When Mr. X began to confide how much he needed them, how alone he was, how each of them was the only bright spot in his day, the women were the ones who tried to put the brakes on, telling him it was a bit premature to imagine a monogamous relationship with a modem-based lover. But Mr. X pressed on, and God, he was irresistible. If he wanted to make them feel like they were the only ones in the world, if that was what he needed, what was the point in constantly refusing or criticizing him? He gave them fantastic sex. It was just delicious.

Of course, each woman, separately, began to make plans to meet Mr. X in person. He lived on the other side of the country from both of them. He admitted, with great chagrin, that he wasn't rolling in dough. But money was not going to stand in the way! Once a woman is really and truly sexually aroused, there is nothing, NOTHING that will stand in her path to satisfaction.

I didn't have any sense of where this story was heading until Gloria and Em mentioned money. It made me shudder, of course; he had them completely in his trust. Of course, they would send money for a flight to their hometowns, and why not pick up his phone and dentist bills while they were at it? I knew they weren't stupid; this happens in real flesh relationships all the time, and it's humiliating whether there's new technology involved or not.

Up to this point, each woman only knew of her "monogamous" tele-relationship to Mr. X. Then, one day, he didn't call, didn't e-mail, didn't respond to a single bloody message. Their checks had been cashed, and there was nothing else left to prove he even existed. Both women were terribly hurt, and after licking their wounds alone for a while, one woman went online and cried her heart out in a private love-life discussion area. Em, reading Gloria's blow-by-blow descriptions, got a creepy feeling. She sent Gloria e-mail, expressing how eerily familiar this story sounded—"What is YOUR guy's name, anyhow?" They both fizzled into white-hot steam as they typed it in together.

Em and Gloria developed a hunch that they might not be the only ones involved—hence the introduction of the "That Greasy Bastard" subject area. They put out their story and a call: Were there any other women on the WELL to whom this sort of thing had happened? I thought they were brave, doing the right thing, but that they were also a little pathetic. I congratulated myself for not wearing the sort of psychic "FUCK ME, KICK ME" sign on my back that seems to attract this kind of attention. Women can be such suckers!

Other women in the topic were not as aloof as I. It started to seem like either there were a lot of these lying cads on line or that this ONE man had really been busy. The women posting in the topic felt, hey, let's name names here: this man doesn't deserve any discretion, none. Usually, it is strict online etiquette to never mention someone's name in gossip or rumors or love life adventures, but a consensus was developing that that was going to be the first exception.

My imagination was running wild. From Gloria and Em's description so far, I could tell he was somebody who posted frequently in the popular culture spots on the WELL, and I laughed myself silly imagining who it could be. The activist WELL women decided, yep, it was time to throw in this guy's towel, he's not going to drown another one. They took a deep breath and spelled his name out loud and clear: Carl Bailey Jones.

Jesus Christ. I had just fucked that man two months earlier in New York City.

I'll Never Forget You

IN TODAY'S POLITICAL CLIMATE, sex with a stranger can be extraordinarily satisfying. The highly condemned "anonymous" sex—with someone whose name you can't remember afterward, or perhaps only for forty-eight hours—cannot only result in an orgasm or two, but can be a meeting of spirit and body, a kinship that's all the more intense because it happens so fast. Sex with a stranger persists, despite all its risks, because there is a special kind of lust that only happens when one's lover is unfamiliar—and also because, among all the regrets and uncertainty of picking someone out of the blue, there is the occasional "Where have you been all my life?", the "I'll never forget you," in which "you" means something much deeper than a last name.

I mention the political climate because there's a cloud of shame and accusation hanging around anonymous sex; it's purported to be at the bottom of spreading nasty diseases, so much so that people imagine their funeral at the end of every anonymous sex encounter. Sex with strangers is equated with promiscuity—an ugly word in itself, since it assumes there is some quantity of sex that is TOO much. Too many people having too much sex with each other equals no damn good.

227

Finally, sex with strangers is often thought of badly because it's assumed that you and the "stranger" don't care about each other, that it's cold and unfeeling and exploitative because you don't know where they work or what their mother does or what books have influenced them. This is probably the most ironic myth of all about anonymous sex—that it lacks intimacy—since having sex with someone you've never known before will often leave you with a secret about them that no one else in their familiar life could ever guess. It's similar to being stuck in the elevator with a stranger, when they blurt out a story to you and you confide likewise in them. Then the elevator is fixed and you walk out, never to see that soul again yet feeling intensely grateful to them.

Sex with strangers is not reliably orgasmic, or happy, or spiritually uplifting; in fact, it can be the absolute opposite. But I would say that it is nearly always intimate, because it is very rare to fuck someone for the first time without being, if only for a moment, scared.

I had sex one afternoon, in New York City, with the man who I later learned was the notorious Mr. X, and it was not good sex, but it was definitely intimate. Like the other women who had received messages from him on their computers, I had become fond of this man who wrote me these admiring and crushed-out letters. He seemed to have read all my books, he knew his way around the feminist sex debates, he was funny, we had some similar tastes in music and movies. Unlike the other women he was corresponding with, I was rather accustomed to this sort of attention, because having a public persona attracts all kinds of letters, phone calls, and unsolicited gifts. I'm always truly touched when someone writes me a letter telling me how my work has influenced them or about experiences they've had that reflect my own.

So when Carl wrote me I was flattered, I was compassionate, but I did not think we had something special going on. I did not long to hear from him, although it was pleasant when I did. When I announced I was going on a book tour that would end in New York, he said we had to meet, this was our big chance. So I agreed, both because of his enthusiastic persistence and also because of the novel prospect of meeting someone face-to-face that I'd gotten to know online. I'd never done that before. I couldn't help but wonder if he was cute. He knew what I looked like from my book covers, but I hoped he didn't think I walked around like that, in latex and hair spray. The anticipation was quite titillating.

Three months and fifteen cities later, I was in New York, the last stop of my book tour. I wanted to lay down my bags and die. If there was a Celebrity Correspondence Course, there would be a chapter that tells you that the biggest challenge a touring artist faces is not selling their work—it's avoiding total physical collapse. The whole structure of book tours is designed for androids, not flesh and blood. You can't eat, sleep, or breathe normally, and every airport brings a new round of germs to destroy what little immune system you have left. By the time I got to New York, I had bronchitis, diarrhea, a migraine, and sciatica. I know it sounds like I'm geriatric, but I was a formerly healthy strapping young woman.

I called Carl the morning of our brunch date and told him, "Look, I'm dead, this is me speaking to you from a coffin being lowered into the ground—we'll have to take a rain check."

Disappointed, he protested, saying, "Isn't there anything I can do for you, bring to you?"—and he said it so winsomely I felt a little sadistic.

"Okay," I said, "if you're really serious, this is what I want: Kaopectate, a carton of cooked Chinese rice, a jar of applesauce, Advil, and Premium saltine crackers. You have to be willing to just hand it to me through the door and then leave."

He said it would be his honor to hand me Kaopectate and rice through the door, and that he was on his way right that minute from New Jersey.

Cyber Cad would have been called Cyber Puppy if everyone on the WELL could have seen his face. As soon as I looked through the peephole at him clutching his little paper bag of supplies, I knew I'd let him in the door. He wasn't cute and he wasn't ugly, he was just a dear boy on a mission of mercy, and he deserved my gratitude.

I opened the door. I looked like shit. He looked at me like I was a goddess. I took the groceries out of his arms and embraced him. Suddenly I realized that on top of every other rotten symptom I was experiencing, I was the loneliest girl in the world in a crummy hotel room.

I was the most blunt I've ever been, as I touched his chin with my fingers: "Do you want to get it on?" He sank his head into my breasts. I had that intensely feminine rush—I have made someone happy—and then I wondered, "Will he make me feel that way too?"

My rush bowled us both over, and it didn't last long. It's funny how I moved completely across the gender role divide: after I came, I felt like such a guy, I couldn't get him out of the room fast enough. He wanted to linger, and I wanted to be alone with my Saltines—no hard feelings, just get out, out, out!

I don't know exactly what made me feel so cold. It was his touch, not what he said. The spell of his online persona had been broken. He was not sexually sophisticated; in fact, he was strangely behind the times. He wasn't accustomed to using condoms. What did he think, I was going to have a baby with him? He relished me going down on him, but clearly was never going to go down on me. The puppy stuff was for real. He was reckless and awkward and absorbed with his bone. It was funny, because even though I didn't fake an orgasm—I could've come rubbing up against the fridge, I'd been alone for so long—I had to fake everything else, because he was so "WOW ISN'T THIS INCREDIBLE YOU'VE CHANGED MY LIFE!" My reaction was, at best, "Gee, that's nice, I really have to go to sleep now."

I hoped I hadn't been downright rude; I argued it back and forth in my head. I had seduced him straight out, so it wasn't like he'd taken advantage of me—maybe I'd been the exploiter. But I had been direct, hadn't I? And I'd only said, "Let's get it on," not "Let's go steady." I didn't offer him romance, just consensuality and lust, and I resented him for trying to make a honeymoon out of it.

Later, when Carl's fame as Multi-Monogamy Man began to spread, I realized this was just his m.o.—fuck the girl and get her undying loyalty, too. None of the women he initially seduced online wanted a primary relationship—they were entirely enamored of the thrill. He was the one who pushed for secrecy, fidelity, romantic consumption.

Carl sent swoony e-mail to me for days after our one-night stand, and I felt plenty guilty. Unlike the other WELL women, I didn't want to have another rendezvous, and I was kicking myself for not having the guts to be blunt about it.

Luckily, Carl changed his course with me one day; he asked me to read a detective novel he'd just written and sent to his agent. He told me it was rather controversial, because it dealt with the S/M underworld, and his concern was that this element would prevent him from getting a fair reading.

I was flat on my back with post–book tour pneumonia, so when his manuscript arrived, I was so bored and moody that I thought, "Well, why not?" I read the whole thing in bed that afternoon. It opened like typical private-eye pulp you'd pick up at the airport, with Carl taking on the voice and alter ego of his gumshoe hero.

The detective was decidedly a hero, a good guy investigating the death of a young woman who'd split on her respectable family and become a dominatrix in a local brothel. Boy, if he thought this was a controversial plot, he had missed out on a lot of private dick novels. Then, in his conclusion, something bizarre happened: the detective finds out who committed the murders, but instead of arresting the perp, he frames an innocent man who is convicted and goes to the pokey forever. The innocent man is an unsavory character in the eyes of our hero—he is a religious conservative—but he has never killed anyone.

I was shocked by this entirely unexpected twist in the plot. As I wrote in my response to Carl, I could go for the detective turning out to be a guy who would pull something like this, but he could not present his man as Mr. Clean Morally Unambivalent and then spring a double-cross on the reader like that. I told him I ended up feeling sorry for the right-wing preacher who the hero/author so obviously loathed.

Carl sent me back his last and weirdest message. He said he didn't understand what I thought the detective had done wrong. Famous last words.

Meanwhile, back at the cyber ranch, many of the women who had been active on the topic of "That Greasy Bastard" decided to take this mess public, to the general news area of the WELL. They started a topic called "Do You Know This Cyber Scam Artist?" They said it wasn't a proud moment, but this is what happened to us—this creep is out of control, and the only way to stop him is to ask other women to come forward who think they've been victims of the same scam.

"This is not normal courtship behavior," wrote one of the women. "This man has acted deceitfully and hurtfully, in a calculated, systematic way . . . please be aware of this person and his modus operandi."

The Cyber Cad announcement prompted the longest and most personal argument I have ever seen, on line or off. First of all, other women came forward—including me, ultimately. One woman revealed that she'd been a lesbian for dog-years, but this guy got her hooked by e-mail, and before you knew it, she was looking forward to having phone sex with him every morning from eight to ten—she was drooling. Next thing you know, she was getting ready to send him money by Western Union to pay his bills. She said it was the best sex she'd ever had.

One of the original posters confided that the only reason she hadn't paid for his plane ticket was that she just wanted to lose a few more pounds before she met him. That made me cry. She said phone sex with him was the best sex she'd ever had. Another woman HAD paid for half his plane fare and also raved about the sex. I had to pinch myself, wondering, how can this be the same guy? I missed out!

Other people asked the perfectly reasonable question: When did this guy have time to take a shit?! He had regular hours with all his lovers, and he told each one that she was his lifeline, his angel in a storm.

Most people who converse in online services are men; the debate over Mr. Cyber Cad took place between a dozen or so women and hundreds of guys. The men were quite divided in their responses. Some said, "Hang 'im high, close his account." Other men were at pains to defend their gender, to say that this guy was an aberration. Some felt he'd started out innocently, and that only a fine line marked when and where he'd gone too far.

The most notorious posts from any one man, however, were from Tom Mandel, who said—with not one whit of apprehension—that if the girls wanted to play a game of hearts and romance, then they could damn well take care of themselves—stop whining, stop asking for protection or punishments. He was characteristically harsh—he didn't know Cyber Cad and didn't particularly want to. While other people in the discussion began to explore the exact psychological definition of a sociopath, Mandel was taking on all of womankind.

I was impressed with Tom's criticism, but I thought he should apply it across the board. These women had taken their lumps, they had examined themselves, and now they were dishing it right back out. Yes, this was a weenie roast, and so what? Carl had had his dick in the fire all along. I didn't feel sorry for the guy, and I was curious about this sociopath stuff as well. I kept thinking about his novel, and how he didn't understand what his detective had done wrong.

I think Carl lived his own soap opera to its logical conclusion; his own plight and pathos were uppermost in his mind, and he couldn't see anybody else. Meanwhile, women in general, not just on the WELL, are starved for good sex—it's a pandemic situation—and like anyone who has been denied the essentials, they have a hard time staying prudent when the good stuff finally starts trickling down. I may have missed the supersonic sex that Carl supposedly had to offer, but I HAVE made a complete idiot out of myself chasing after someone who turned me on to my body and opened up the sexual store for me. Some of these promising individuals turned out to be pricks, some princes. Luckily, these encounters happened when I was younger and broke; I didn't have any money for anyone to con me out of, but I'm sure in a vulnerable moment one of them could have asked me to rob a bank. Women are so sexually repressed that no one should be surprised if they go haywire when the lid comes off. We have a lot of catching up to do.

Hundreds of people posted outrage of one sort or another in the Cyber Cad topic area before someone finally asked, Well, where the fuck is he? Where is Cyber Cad? How could he not know that he was being crucified?

Some lurker who hardly ever said a word in any discussion came out of the corner like a little mouse. "He's with my girlfriend, Linda. They went camping in the Sierras together about a week ago." There was a moment of silence as everyone contemplated the notion of Cyber Cad being unavailable to technology.

Someone from the WELL office said, look, it's a moot point whether to throw him off the service, because he hasn't paid his bill in months, he's already suspended, and he's been using other people's accounts for any activity he's been posting.

Some people were ready to start a search party for the presumably unsuspecting Linda. Others said there was no way she could be separated from her cash in the Sierras, so just leave them alone. Some of the women involved were now more angry at Tom and his allies than they were at Cyber Cad; they withdrew from the discussion and in some cases scribbled out their previous entries. That part made me the saddest yet, witnessing how women who had shown a lot of guts in sharing their stories would decide it wasn't worth being the political dartboard for cynics, misogynists, and tabloid headliners. I understand how hard it is to answer the constant criticisms—it was like, hey, I hope you never get your heart broken by a bastard, because you'll never forgive yourself. Then I wondered if Tom had had HIS heart broken, and his lack of sympathy was the result. It was all terribly personal, and when people started to erase their most personal comments, the discussion lost its belly.

Carl finally did crawl out of his sleeping bag and return to his modem. It was anticlimactic. He was taken aback; he felt wronged, didn't think he'd done anything so bad. "It is quite clear to me that I am a lightning rod for some generalized female anger about men . . . the cyber world is the same as the real world . . . I should have realized the exact same standards should have applied."

The weirdest part about Carl's comments were that they didn't fit into the commune that our WELL discussion had become. While other postings had moved me to tears or laughter or fury—and believe me, when I wanted to strangle Tom Mandel, I could feel every other woman's hands reaching out to do the same—Carl's comments were very solitary, like he was addressing a group of strangers. We had all "had sex" with Carl Bailey Jones, and he couldn't remember our names, because his own mystery melodrama loomed larger than any of our reactions.

It was a strange blind date for me. No one died, no one got a disease; nonetheless, it was risky. I remember what Carl tasted like, how much the Saltines and applesauce made me feel better—and how, when I read the last chapter of his detective novel, I thought, well, you can just never tell about people, can you?

Sources

Adam Film World Guide Directory of Adult Films, compiled by Jeremy Stone, Knight Publications, Los Angeles: 1996.

"America Online Reverses Ban on 'Breast'," *Associated Press:* December 2, 1995.

The Antioch College Sexual Offense Policy, Antioch College, Yellow Springs, OH: 1993.

Bright, Susie, "The Prime of Miss Kitty MacKinnon," *Susie Bright's Sexwise.* Cleis Press, Pittsburgh: 1995.

Chauncey, George, Jr., "The Post-War Sex Crime Panic," *True Stories from the American Past,* edited by William Graebner, McGraw-Hill, New York: 1993.

Chinn, Steven, "Oregon Killing Suspect: Murder's 'Interesting'," *San Francisco Examiner:* December 17, 1995.

Deakin, Thomas, *F.B.I. Law Enforcement Bulletin,* vol. 54, no. 8: August 1985.

Dodson, Betty, *Sex for One,* Crown Quality Paperback, New York: 1986.

Ellis, Kate, Beth Jaker, Nan D. Hunter, Barbara O'Dair, and Abbey Tallmer, *Caught Looking: Feminism, Pornography, and Censorship,* Long River Books, East Haven, CT: 1986.

Godwin, Mike, "The Rimmjob," *Penthouse:* September 1996.

Good Vibrations Sexuality Library catalog, Open Enterprises, San Francisco: 1996.

Highleyman, Liz, "New Internet Censorship Legislation Proposed," *San Francisco Bay Times:* December 28, 1995.

Holliday, Jim, *Only the Best: Jim Holliday's Adult Video Almanac and Trivia Treasury,* Cal Vista, Van Nuys: 1986.

Kanaley, Reid, "Free Speech Activists Decry Internet 'Censorship' in New Telecom Law," *The Philadelphia Inquirer:* February 8, 1996.

Lean, Marcelle, "Board Games, or I was a Member of the Ontario Film Review Board," *Border/Lines: Canada's Magazine of Cultural Studies,* No. 31: 1993/94.

Males, Mike, "Sex Survey's 'Warm Oatmeal' Sold as Solid Social Science," *Extra:* January/February 1995, pp. 24–26.

McDonnell, Evelyn, "Why I Wore a Gorilla Mask at My Wedding," *Resistor* 1, no. 1, 1996.

McDonnell, Evelyn, and Lee Foust, "The Wedding Manifesto," *Resistor* 1, no. 1, 1996.

McMillan, Dennis, "Everything You Always Wanted to Know About Oral Sex," *San Francisco Bay Times:* January 25, 1996.

Morin, Jack, *The Erotic Mind,* HarperCollins, New York: 1995.

Ogden, Katherine, "Play Stresses 'No Sex Is Safest Sex'," *Middletown Press,* Middletown, CT: March 1995.

Penley, Constance, "Crackers and Whackers: 'The White Trashing of Porn'," *White Trash,* edited by Annalee Newitz and Matt Wray, Routledge, New York: 1996.

Powers, Ann, "Queer in the Streets, Straight in the Sheets: Notes on Passing," *Surface Tension,* edited by Meg Daly, Touchstone, New York: 1996.

Rimm, Martin, *The Pornographer's Handbook: How to Exploit Women, Dupe Men, and Make Lots of Money,* Usenet: 1995.

"Savannah's Suicide," *Rolling Stone:* October 20, 1994.

Rowberry, John, *Gay Video: A Guide to Erotica,* Gay Sunshine Press, San Francisco: 1986

Schwartz, John, "On-Line Lothario's Antics Prompt Debate on Cyber-Age Ethics," *The Washington Post:* July 7, 1993.

SelfLoving, a video directed by Betty Dodson, produced by Betty Dodson Productions: 1992.

Thomas, Trish, "Me and the Boys," *The Best American Erotica 1993,* edited by Susie Bright, Scribner, New York: 1993.

Whitlock, Jason, "Get the Message, People," *Santa Cruz Sentinel:* February 13, 1996. Originally published in *Kansas City Star.*

Winkes, Cathy, and Anne Semans, *The Good Vibrations Book of Sex,* Cleis Press, Pittsburgh: 1994.

Zilbergeld, Bernie, *The New Male Sexuality,* Bantam, New York: 1992.

Index